WILLIAM BUTLER YEATS

By

John H. Hackett POLLOCK

(an pilibín)

LONDON : GERALD DUCKWORTH & CO., LIMITED
DUBLIN : THE TALBOT PRESS, LIMITED

First Published 1935

Made in Ireland at
The Talbot Press
Dublin

TO THE MEMORY OF
MY FATHER

I HAVE to express my indebtedness to Messrs. Macmillan for their courtesy and generosity in the matter of quotations; which I am aware are very much more numerous than is usual in a work of this kind; but to attempt to substitute a clumsy and inadequate personal paraphrase for the poet's perfect utterance would appear to me to partake of the nature of an impertinence. I may add that in the case of *The Man who Dreamed of Fairy Land* and in *The Two Trees*, I have adhered to the earlier versions of these poems—an adherence which I justify upon the grounds of a quarter of a century's enchanted familiarity.

FOREWORD

LIONEL JOHNSON, in his *Art of Thomas Hardy*,
stressed the inevitable delicacy and difficulty in
dealing critically with the work of a living author.
If so admirable an authority, whose literary
activity corresponded with a relatively stable social
and political phase, might feel sensitive in such
an undertaking, how much more onerous appears
the task of the present writer. No artist may be
completely abstracted from the background
against which he moves, be the points of contact
with that background never so few: and if such
background change and reform approximately
every decade, as has been practically the case in
Ireland during Dr. Yeats's career, the task of
arriving at a complete and rounded estimate is
not rendered any the easier. Granted that such
an argument might be strenuously resisted by no
less an authority than Dr. Yeats himself: granted
that he may lay claim to be considered as an
artist sole, self-contained and self-sufficient:
nevertheless, he may hardly expect exemption
from conditions which govern our appreciation of
such figures as Shakespeare, Milton or Shelley.
A knowledge of the historical circumstances of
the Elizabethan period is necessary before we
can account for the florid exuberance, the ebullient

7

vitality of the first: the brief English republican experiment unquestionably influenced the second in his capacity as poet: while the intoxicated and intoxicating ideal humanism of the last finds its logical explanation in the fall of the Bastille. The outcome of such train of thought might suggest that the poet is, or at all events can be, the child of his age: be this as it may, Shelley has passionately repudiated the thesis that his own age can ever be competent to assess the work of any particular poet: which reflection must operate as a further deterrent in projects like the present. Perspective, then, is essential to accurate artistic estimate; and perspective is lamentably fore-shortened in Ireland. Curiously enough, it is more than possible that the peculiar intellectual isolation—not to say egoism—of Dr. Yeats, which has progressively increased of later years, may prove to be a dissatisfied personal reaction to a perpetual political and social mutability: if this be granted as plausible, it serves but to confirm my original proposition that no artist, however introverted, can reasonably lay claim to be divorced from the circumstances of his own particular period. Lastly, in Dr. Yeats's case, the circumstances in question are sufficiently recent and highly coloured to reasonably justify an omission of them here: thus, the object of the present brief and inadequate survey may be permitted to remain purely and solely critical, a scope which would probably be endorsed by the subject himself.

8

WILLIAM BUTLER YEATS

I.

UNTIL comparatively recently, speaking in a broad, historical sense, the idea of Irish poetry was inextricably associated with the verses of Thomas Moore; even down to the closing days of that presently too much derided Victorian epoch, people existed who would select him as our national poet. The grounds of such a choice are to-day admittedly insufficient, and Moore is reaching a nadir of literary reputation in exact inverse proportion to his original zenith: in this regard, curiously resembling his pinchbeck contemporary Byron. With one exquisite exception, the lines commencing: " At the mid-hour of night, when stars are weeping," Moore's verses are conspicuously lacking in distinction, individuality, or atmosphere; three qualities reasonably to be expected from any writer laying claim to be a poet representative of a nation. They might with equal justice be ascribed to an Englishman, Welshman, or Scotchman, rather than to an Irishman: rhetoric too frequently takes the place of inspiration, while sentimentality deputises for

9

passion.   His influence upon his successors was
great, however, and, with the brilliant exception
of Mangan, their poetry was invariably tinged
with an intolerable provincialism, as witness the
bulk of the work of such supposedly representative Irish verse-writers as Griffin, Davis, or, in
his lyrics, at all events, the otherwise superior
Ferguson.   Possibly the most widely known lines
of Moore are those in which he attempts to
celebrate the Vale of Avoca in terms suitable for
a guide-book of his period :

> " There is not in the wide world a valley so sweet
>   As that vale in whose bosom the bright waters
>   meet.
>   Oh! the last days of feeling and life must
>   depart
>   Ere the bloom of that valley shall fade from
>   my heart."

Whatever merit these lines actually possess does
not consist in any adequate evocation of the Vale
of Avoca, or, indeed, of any other Irish scene.
To experience such evocation one turns to the
following :

> " Shanwalla, where a willow-bordered pond
>   Gathers the wild-duck from the winter's dawn,"

to instinctively acknowledge, moreover, the per-
suasive thrill of genius.

These lines, from the dedication of *The
Shadowy Waters* might be accepted by a superficial reader as spontaneous and unpremeditated :

but the genius of Yeats has always been increas-
ingly deliberate and self-conscious. If one turns
to that essay in *Ideas of Good and Evil*, entitled
What is Popular Poetry? written early in his
literary career, one finds laid down as a personal
artistic canon: " one's verse should hold, as in
a mirror, the colour of one's own climate and
scenery." Obedient to a self-imposed ordinance,
the same principle finds more perfect and complete
expression in lines from that book so characteristic
of his later period, *The Wild Swans at Coole :*

" *We dreamed that a great painter had been born*
   To cold Clare rock, and Galway rock and thorn,
   To that stern colour and that delicate line
   That are our secret discipline."

Stern colour—delicate line—secret discipline; an
epitome of the later art of William Butler Yeats
at his best, which may fairly render further attempts at analysis or exposition superfluous.

An artistic conscience, then, a scrupulosity as
regards the precise word or phrase in which to
convey an exact impression, has been not the least
contribution of Yeats to Anglo-Irish letters; a
contribution all the more precious because of its
conspicuous absence in those writers of an earlier
period already referred to. The accusation of
provincialism against many of our supposedly
representative poets I propose to staunchly main-
tain; while to that personal verdict I will add a
rider: the majority of them are, in addition,

slovenly; frequently, if not always, content with the second-best words or phrases, merely because they come unbidden to the mind. No one amongst these versifiers could ever have attained to that certainty of touch which frequently characterises Yeats. To select an example from amongst many, one has but to repeat and consider the first verse from *The Rose of the World:*

> " *Who dreamed that beauty passes like a dream?*
> *For these red lips, with all their mournful pride,*
> *Mournful that no new wonder may betide,*
> *Troy passed away in one high funeral gleam,*
> *And Usna's children died.*"

Beyond a doubt, any other writer might have been content with some more obvious term than that of *high;* say *wild*, or *bright*, or *fierce*. Substitute any of these three, and read the lines again, preferably aloud: the effect is indefinably weakened; whereas, by the employment of that simple monosyllable *high*, Yeats provides us, as it were, with a glimpse of the beauty of Helen, the stature of Hecuba, the fall of the great tower —even all the passionate lamentation of *The Trojan Women* of Euripides. Again, one is conscious of the thrill of genius as opposed to the facility of talent. Take another example, the farewell of Countess Cathleen to Oona and Aleel:

> " *Bend down your faces, Oona and Aleel:*
> *I gaze upon them as the swallow gazes*
> *Upon the nest under the eave, before*
> *He wander the loud waters.*"

The employment of the adjective *loud*, rather than some such more familiar epithet as *waste* or *wild*, justifies one in applying to the poet's selection, in this particular instance, the term *inevitable*. Nor may these points be considered in the light of mere happy verbal accidents: it is a question of conscious selection, of deliberate choice; and is not an infinite capacity for taking pains one of the definitions of genius?

The poetry of Yeats, then, may claim to be the first English poetry in Ireland for close upon a century to exhibit the quality of a deliberate search for style; a quest which has culminated in his later work in an austere economy of phrase without parallel among contemporary poets. The besetting literary sin of most young poets is luxuriance: and Yeats himself was not entirely exempt from this failing in his earlier phase. Open his first considerable poem, *The Wanderings of Oisin*, at random:

" *And with low murmurs we rode on,*
Where many a trumpet-twisted shell
That in immortal silence sleeps
Dreaming of her own melting hues,
Her golds, her ambers, and her blues,
Pierced with soft lights the shallowing deeps."

Turn now to what is perhaps the most individual of his later achievements, *The Dreaming of the Bones*, from *Four Plays for Dancers*:

> " They've passed the shallow well and the flat
>   stone
> Fouled by the drinking cattle, the narrow lane
> Where mourners for five centuries have carried
> Noble or peasant to his burial; . . . .
> And now they have climbed through the long
>   grassy field
> And passed the ragged thorn-trees and the gap
> In the ancient hedge . . . .
> They are among the stones above the ash
> Above the briar and thorn and the scarce grass."

In the first passage we possess but a cosmopolitan luxuriant fantasy, while the second has the severe compression of a dry-point etching, while conveying a sense of actual beauty, a scenery peculiar to Ireland, to which the former cannot pretend. Yeats has written in *Ireland and the Arts* that it took him years to rid himself of the Italian light of Shelley, but that he has succeeded, and that his style is now himself. " I might have found more," he exclaims again, " had I written in Irish, but I have found a little, and I have found all myself." And lastly, in the lines

> " I said: ' A line will take us hours maybe:
>   Yet if it does not seem a moment's thought,
>   Our stitching and unstitching has been
>   naught,' "

there stands the exacting literary conscience self-confessed, a phenomenon so rare hitherto in Irish letters as to earn for its present exponent the accusation of *poseur*.

In effect, so accustomed have the majority of

our reading public become to the casual methods
of his predecessors, so difficult have they found
it to appreciate his artistic integrity, that Yeats
has fallen under a further suspicion of not being
a *national* poet in any true sense of the term.
Surely such an argument is difficult to sustain
upon an impartial examination of all available
facts. First and last, we possess that little play,
Cathleen-ni-Houlihan, unique in the distinction of
exhibiting artistic excellence associated with public
popularity; and apart from it, throughout the
entire range of his writing, Yeats shares an active
sympathy with our political ideals. Upon almost
the first page of one of his earliest volumes, moreover, we encounter surely an adequate *apologia*
for his personal position :

> " *Know, that I would accounted be*
> *True brother of that company,*
> *Who sang to sweeten Ireland's wrong,*
> *Ballad and story, rann and song;*
> *Nor be I any less of them,*
> *Because the red-rose-bordered hem*
> *Of her, whose history began*
> *Before God made the angelic clan,*
> *Trails all about the written page.*"

Here he asks his public to permit a reconciliation
between their universal political and his more
particular aesthetic ideal. The case is frankly
stated, without equivocation: yet by a large
section of his fellow-countrymen he has been,
and is yet, while to a lesser extent, mistrusted.
Nor will we search the later volumes altogether in

15

vain for further proofs of sympathy with traditional political aspirations. *Red Hanrahan's Song upon Ireland*, with its passionate refrain concerning Cathleen the daughter of Houlihan: " 1913 "—with the melancholy sequence to each verse: " Romantic Ireland's dead and gone—it's with O'Leary in the grave "; and last, but perhaps above all, in that later consummation of his most elaborate yet most purified art, *The Dreaming of the Bones*, the bitter cry of the country boy, returning to Clare-Galway from his part in the Dublin insurrection of 1916: " Oh never, never, may Dermod and Dervorgilla be forgiven !"

But quite apart from identification with the political trend, in matters of atmosphere and topography, which are possibly of even greater aesthetic importance, Yeats has proved himself sufficiently local in his choice to satisfy surely even the most parochial-minded among us. With the exception of excursions into Renaissance Italy and elsewhere—excursions, by the way, usually provoked by a not entirely unreasonable dissatisfaction with his reception nearer home—his scenery is the soil, the water, the superincumbent clouds of Ireland, whose moody temperament he evokes more perfectly than any Irish poet hitherto. Furthermore, the very birds and beasts who figure in his pages are those of our native fields and foreshore. " The three oldest cries—the cry of wind, the cry of water, and the cry of curlew ",

" the wind-borne clamour of the barnacle geese " ;
the raven, " upon whose ancient wing scarcely a
feather lingered " ; " the mountain grass " which
" cannot but keep the form where the mountain
hare has lain " ; the white gull blown by storm
at night, and " thrown between dark furrows upon
the ploughed land " ; each and all of these images
and phenomena are essentially native to that
Ireland which many of us love more passionately
and disinterestedly, it may well be, than any
mere political abstraction. And here again in
this connexion let us disabuse ourselves of any
idea that these things are accidental. It is, finally,
a question of deliberate choice, as any doubter
may satisfy himself by reading once more the
essay entitled *Ireland and the Arts*, in *Ideas of
Good and Evil:* " I am yet jealous for Cuchulain
and for Baile, and for Aillin, and for those gray
mountains that still are lacking their celebration
. . . . the verses, or the stories, or the events that
would make every lake or mountain a man can
see from his own door an excitement to his
imagination." There remains for consideration
the more serious argument that Yeats cannot fairly
claim to be considered an Irish poet, because he
has not written in Gaelic; neither time nor space
permits of present discussion upon this point—
rendered all the more difficult to judge impartially
because of an impassioned bias upon the part of
the several protagonists.

So limited, and as a consequence, so intense, so passionate almost, has been the poet's fidelity, that one may dare surmise that certain localities in Sligo and Clare-Galway will, in the distant future, become places of literary pilgrimage, comparable to Dorset, to Grasmere, to Haworth— even to Stratford-upon-Avon. And if such a service to one's country be not a high and unquestionable form of patriotism some among us must have grievously misunderstood the term. Yet the faint questioning of his credentials, the vague mistrust of his qualifications as an Irish poet, persists; and its presence and persistence, by a strange irony, has proved of more artistic service to Dr. Yeats than might a more widespread popularity. It has converted the originally *objective* artistic impulse which created *The Lake Isle of Innisfree*, *The Stolen Child*, or *Cathleen Ní Houlihan* into the most *subjective* poetic method of this generation; a method which has for outcome *Responsibilities*, *The Wild Swans at Coole*, *The Tower*, and *Four Plays for Dancers*. This is the great division measuring the periods or phases of his art: from *objective diffuseness* to *subjective intensity:* luxuriant extroversion repudiated for austere introversion. The former constitutes his more popular period, the latter, in many eyes, his more enduring and valuable one, which might never have developed had the poet been accepted by an enthusiastic but indiscriminating public. The note of disappointment at

18

his reception, however, commences in *Responsibilities*, deepening in his later work until he finds himself completely isolated in the last, yet with his art purified by that process of intellectual segregation. Yet long before the attainment of that goal his poetry has become bitter in the face of popular misunderstanding of the original aims of the contemporary Irish literary and dramatic movement :

" ' *What have I earned for all that work,' I said,*
' For all that I have done at my own charge?
The daily spite of this unmannerly town,
Where who has served the most is most defamed,
The reputation of his lifetime lost
Between the night and morning.' "

And still more bitter in the lines, *To a friend Whose Work has come to Nothing:*

" *Now all the truth is out,*
Be secret and take defeat
From any brazen throat,
For how can you compete,
Being honour bred, with one
Who, were it proved he lies,
Were neither shamed in his own
Nor in his neighbour's eyes?"

I propose, in effect, to divide the work of William Butler Yeats into three phases : but in doing so, one must always remember that in any vital human process, such as art, all divisions are to some extent arbitrary, and not to be too rigidly applied; overlapping and intermingling are inevitable.

Taken then, for what the artificial schedule is worth, I would consider Yeats firstly in his youthful *objective* phase: secondly, in a phase of disillusion, disappointment, and self-questioning, arising, I believe, from a variety of intimate causes; and lastly, in that period of mature reflection, *subjective* for the most part, in which the poet may be reasonably expected to have finally found himself. And this I hold to be the important point at issue: whether self-realisation and self-expression through the joint media of life and letters, has, in Dr. Yeats's case, been complete, or even adequate to the depth of his temperament, the individual force of his personality.

II.

DR. YEATS has written somewhere that, in his opinion, a man shall find his heaven where he first crept upon the floor: an unconscious paraphrase of Wordsworth's line: " Heaven lies about us in our infancy." In either case, the implied paradise surely suggests a simple *objective* delight in our surroundings, untroubled by question or speculation. It is such an atmosphere, for the most part, that pervades the more representative portion of Yeats's earlier work centred chiefly in Sligo, where so much of his childhood was spent. The very title of that early book: *The Wind among the Reeds*, may well have been suggested by the

country which lies between Upper and Lower
Rosses, which must have been familiar to him in
boyhood. To the north of Rosses Point, behind
that village which Mr. Jack Yeats has quaintly
pictured over the poignant title " Memory
Harbour" as a frontispiece to his brother's
Reveries over Childhood and Youth, lie a group
of some seven or so little lakes, beset with tall
tufted reeds whose whispering to the wind may
be heard even upon the surrounding hills. These
little lakes, with their unique atmosphere and
vague melancholy, figure in the prose study *The
Old Men of the Twilight*, contained in the volume
entitled *The Secret Rose;* and that early book
likewise strays seldom if at all from the county
Sligo. Only those who have explored that locality
can do justice to the delicate elusive quality which
pervades these prose studies, their exact present-
ment of the indefinable emotion produced by the
places themselves. Many, if not most of these
early creations were undertaken in London, or
elsewhere removed from Sligo : that most popular,
and possibly overrated lyric *The Lake Isle of
Innisfree*, being suggested by the tinkle of falling
water overheard in a London shop window : and
it may well be that a passionate unpremeditated
nostalgia was partly operative in the productions
of this period. In or about this time the poet
had written in the *Celtic Twilight:* " Hope and
Memory have one daughter, and her name is Art :
Oh, beloved daughter of Hope and Memory, be

21

with me for a little !'' Nevertheless, the deliberate
intention, the premeditated plan had begun
already to take definite shape and outline within
his mind. '' A national literature that made
Ireland beautiful in the memory, and yet had
been freed from provincialism by an exacting
criticism.'' This and nothing less was the young
man's dream, to which Yeats has adhered for
close upon forty years with unexampled fidelity :
the old man's vision, in basic essentials, but the
mature outcome of that young man's dream.

One among these earlier stories, that entitled
The Wisdom of the King, has always possessed
a particular interest for the present writer. The
king, visited in infancy by the crones of the
great hawk, and who in later life, as a consequence, exhibited hawk's feathers instead of hair :
who is called to the temporalities of a kingdom,
and for many years continues to administer them ;
but in the end abandons the attempt, to pass
beyond men's knowledge : this figure has always
suggested a resemblance to the author himself,
pre-ordained to a life of art, a laborious journey
from objective illusion to subjective reality. Dr.
Yeats has somewhat deprecated these prose
sketches in his later years, as exhibiting the
influence of William Morris : any marked evidence
is perhaps a little to seek; and for some, the
volume of *The Secret Rose*, to which in the only
extant Dublin edition are added the original
version of the *Stories of Red Hanrahan*, takes

precedence, in literary value, even of those early
and more widely known lyric and narrative poems.
This volume has been worked over, re-touched
and re-written, not always with happier results.
While I adhere to the opinion that considers
Yeats's middle and later periods more valuable
and individual than his earlier, I also believe that
to attempt successfully to apply a more advanced
technique to relatively immature work usually
partakes of the nature of futility. The involution
of autumn may not be superimposed upon the
evolution of spring: viewed in relative perspective they fall into sequence and harmony. This
process of re-casting will be found to generally
correspond with the weakening of Yeats's primary
objective inspiration, at a time of personal un-
certainty, dissatisfaction, and moreover, possibly,
poor health.

The art of criticism, practised with integrity,
engenders humility in an impartial critic; try how
he may, his conclusions and deductions fall short
of verity as regards detail and precision. In
common with other writers upon the same subject,
I have deprecated Dr. Yeats's over-conscientious-
ness in the matter of revision, as a form of literary
scrupulosity, which all too frequently fails in its
avowed object of improvement. Nevertheless,
exceptions will be found to prove this irregular
rule: and one of the chief amongst them is to
be found in the *Stories of Red Hanrahan*. In
that entitled *Kathleen the daughter of Hoolihan*,

23

Hanrahan is described as composing a poem which I quote in its entirety for the sake of the subsequent striking contrast upon alteration:

" O tufted reeds, bend low and low in pools on
    the Greenland,
  Under the bitter Black Winds blowing out of
    the left hand!
  Like tufted reeds our courage droops in a Black
    Wind and dies:
  But we have hidden in our hearts the flame out
    of the eyes
      Of Kathleen the daughter of Hoolihan.

  O tattered clouds of the world, call from the
    high Cairn of Maeve
  And shake down thunder on the stones because
    the Red Winds rave!
  Like tattered clouds of the world, passions call
    and our hearts beat:
  But we have all bent low and low, and kissed
    the quiet feet
      Of Kathleen the daughter of Hoolihan.

  O heavy swollen waters, brim the Fall of the
    Oak trees,
  For the Grey Winds are blowing up out of the
    clinging seas!
  Like heavy swollen waters are our bodies and
    our blood:
  But purer than a tall candle before the Blessed
    Rood
      Is Kathleen the daughter of Hoolihan."

Some years later we find an amended version of this poem in the Collected Works under the title

Red Hanrahan's Song about Ireland. Purified
from incoherence and irrelevancies it affords an
outstanding example of Yeats's progress as a
poetic artist, the development of a literary conscience, and a sense of style.

" *The old brown thorn-trees break in two high*
    over Cummen Strand,
  Under a bitter black wind that blows from the
    left hand;
  Our courage breaks like an old tree in a black
    wind and dies,
  But we have hidden in our hearts the flame out
    of the eyes
    Of Cathleen, the daughter of Houlihan.

  The wind has bundled up the clouds high over
    Knocknarea,
  And thrown the thunder on the stones for all
    that Maeve can say.
  Angers that are like noisy clouds have set our
    hearts abeat;
  But we have all bent low and low and kissed
    the quiet feet
    Of Cathleen, the daughter of Houlihan.

  The yellow pool has overflowed high up on
    Clooth-na-Bare,
  For the wet winds are blowing out of the cling-
    ing air;
  Like heavy flooded waters our bodies and our
    blood;
  But purer than a tall candle before the Holy
    Rood
    Is Cathleen, the daughter of Houlihan."

Under the influence of the pruning-knife, the

25

vague diffusion of the earlier version has been removed, and replaced by a spare severity, an approach to that *stern colour*, *delicate line* and *secret discipline* to which allusion has already been made.

In the beginning of the human embryo certain rudimentary structures appear as prototypes of permanent features in the fully developed individual: a similar process occurs in art; in consequence, one of the important, and frequently difficult duties of the critic consists in tracing backward to the germ definite characteristics of artistic maturity. I have already stressed, and would stress again, the gradual transition of Dr. Yeats's art from objectivity to subjectivity: I have emphasised, in addition, the overlapping and intermingling of all phases of human activity. Thus, at a time when the poet was primarily endeavouring to celebrate those hitherto neglected grey mountains of Sligo, a preoccupation with an absolute abstract principle of Beauty had already awakened, and was at work within him. Had he not himself foreseen such increasing preoccupation? Had he not anticipated the suspicion, not to say hostility that such preoccupation must engender in a community which, as he says himself "was engaged, one half in a struggle for existence, the other in a political struggle"? Had he had not written his own passionate apologia, already quoted:

" Nor be I any less of them,
Because the red-rose-bordered hem
Of her, whose history began
Before God made the angelic clan,
Trails all about the written page "?

Suddenly among the celebration of those grey
hills of Knocknarea and Ben Bulben, those dove-
grey sands of Lissadell, arises that pale, luminous
figure, lovable only for herself, and in herself,
who appeared as Cleena of the Wave to Hanrahan,
in the dreams of his half-drunken sleep:

" We and the labouring world are passing by;
Amid men's souls, that waver and give place,
Like the pale waters in their wintry race,
Under the passing stars, foam of the sky,
Lives on this lonely face.

Bow down, archangels, in your dim abode:
Before you were, or any hearts to beat,
Weary and kind one lingered by His seat;
He made the world to be a grassy road
Before her wandering feet."

Or again, a variant upon the same essential
theme:

" Red Rose, proud Rose, sad Rose of all my
days!
Come near me, while I sing the ancient ways:
. . . .
Come near, that no more blinded by man's fate,
I find, under the boughs of love and hate,
In all poor foolish things that live a day,
Eternal beauty wandering on her way."

27

Even at the moment of evanescent love, he reaches from a finite ardour to the infinite:

> " *When my arms wrap you round I press*
> *My heart upon the loveliness*
> *That has long faded from the world.*"

And again, he realises that love will turn ultimately from the mere ephemeral objective vehicle to the primal source of Beauty:

> " *How many loved your moments of glad grace,*
> *And loved your beauty with love false or true;*
> *But one man loved the pilgrim soul in you,*
> *And loved the sorrows of your changing face.*"

Yet even in the face of such spiritual passion, he concludes:

> *And bending down beside the glowing bars,*
> *Murmur, a little sadly, how love fled*
> *And paced upon the mountains overhead*
> *And hid his face amid a crowd of stars.*"

Has not his contemporary and companion, " A.E.," likewise written:

> " *A vast desire awakes and grows into forget-*
> *fulness of thee*"?

The introduction of this partly Platonic mystical principle into the art of Yeats, its permeation therein, lifts the bulk of his less popular work into the rank of the greater poets, placing it, with an admitted difference, close to the *Vita*

28

Nuova of Dante, *The Epipsychidion* of Shelley, *The Soul's Beauty* of Dante Gabriel Rossetti. It endows some of his best poetry with a peculiar quality of dedication, almost akin to religious preoccupation: analagous at moments to that *itinerarium mentis ad Deum*, a study proper to the mystical theologian. So much is this the case, that for some, at all events, Dr. Yeats's present, and apparently final philosophic position appears inadequate, and his esoteric adherence to partake somewhat of the nature of an anti-climax. A few may recall, with a due sense of its inapplicability, the phrase of Matthew Arnold concerning Joubert: " Because he sincerely loved light, and did not prefer to it any little private darkness of his own —he found Light."

The subjective germ, then, may be considered present in Dr. Yeats's work from the commencement; that he was personally conscious of a disturbed mental equilibrium may, I think, be inferred from a consideration of certain poems. The " man whom sorrow named his friend " : who wandered upon a shore which inevitably suggests the strand at Rosses : who sought for comfort from the stars who only laughed and sang among themselves: to whom the waves, " rolling along in dreams from hill to hill," were indifferent : to whose grief the dewdrops were deaf, " for they are always listening, the dewdrops, to the sound of their own dropping "; and who in despair :

29

" Sought once again the shore, and found a shell,
  And thought, ' I will my heavy story tell
  Till my own words, re-echoing, shall send
  Their sadness through a hollow, pearly heart;
  And my own tale again for me shall sing,
  And my own whispering words be comforting,
  And lo, my ancient burden may depart.'
  Then he sang softly nigh the pearly rim;
  But the sad dweller by the sea-ways lone
  Changed all he sang to inarticulate moan
  Among her wildering whirls, forgetting him."

Have we not here a suggestion that to the brood-
ing introverted mind, not even the objectivisation
of art can afford an adequate relief? Again in *The
Madness of King Goll* is presented the triumph
of subjectivity over the simple objective mind and
nature of a warring king; and last, in point of
consideration, but possibly first in merit stands
The Man who dreamed of Fairyland. Dr. Yeats,
at the outset, in *The Hosting of the Sidhe*, had
already written :

" And if any gaze on our rushing band,
  We come between him and the deed of his
    hand,
  We come between him and the hope of his
    heart."

The longer poem is but an elaboration of these
lines : it is of peculiar interest because of its
subjective tendency linked to topographical
atmosphere derived from Rosses and the immediate neighbourhood, and shows as in a picture
of exquisite fragility and melancholy, the poet

30

standing to some extent, at the parting of the artistic ways.

" *He stood among a crowd at Drumahair;*
  His heart hung all upon a silken dress,
  And he had known at last some tenderness,
  Before earth made of him her sleepy care;
  But when a man poured fish into a pile,
  It seemed they raised their little silver heads,
  And sang how day a Druid twilight sheds
  Upon a dim, green, well-beloved isle,
  Where people love beside star-laden seas; . . . .
  The singing shook him out of his new ease . . . .

  He wandered by the sands of Lissadell;
  His mind ran all on money cares and fears,
  And he had known at last some prudent years
  Before they heaped his grave under the hill;
  But while he passed before a plashy place,
  A lug-worm with its grey and muddy mouth
  Sang how somewhere to north or west or south
  There dwelt a gay, exulting, gentle race . . . .
  And at that singing he was no more wise.

  He slept under the hill of Lugnagall:
  And might have known at last unhaunted sleep
  Under that cold and vapour-turbaned steep,
  Now that old earth had taken man and all,—
  Were not the worms that spired about his bones
  A-telling with their low and reedy cry,
  Of how God leans his hands out of the sky,
  To bless that isle with honey in His tones:
  That none may feel the power of squall and
      wave,
  And no one any leaf-crowned dancer miss
  Until He burn up Nature with a kiss:
  The man has found no comfort in the grave."

31

Here again, the trend of thought in these poems finds a curious condensation in the lines by "A. E.":

> "What of all the will to do?
> It has vanished long ago
> Since an arrow pierced it through
> From the Almighty archer's bow."

So we come by these unravelled threads of hope and memory to that poem entitled *The Two Trees*, with its praise of inner quietism and subjectivity and repudiation of externals:—

> "Beloved, gaze in thine own heart,
> The holy tree is growing there;
> From joy the holy branches start,
> And all the trembling flowers they bear.
> The changing colours of its fruit
> Have dowered the stars with merry light:
> The surety of its hidden root
> Has planted quiet in the night;
> The shaking of its leafy head
> Has given the waves their melody,
> And made my lips and music wed,
> Murmuring a wizard song for thee . . . .
>
> Gaze no more in the bitter glass
> The demons with their subtle guile,
> Lift up before us when they pass,
> Or only gaze a little while;
> For there a fatal image grows,
> With broken boughs, and blackened leaves,
> And roots half-hidden under snows
> Driven by a storm that ever grieves.
> For all things turn to barrenness
> In the dim glass the demons hold,
> The glass of outer weariness,
> Made when God slept in times of old." . . . .

Has not Shelley, whose influence Dr. Yeats admits, likewise written:

*" Where is the Beauty, Love, and Truth we seek
But in our minds?"*

And has not an even higher authority than either of these given us the unquestionable assurance that the kingdom of God is within us? " Look in your heart and write " is a time-honoured literary precept: before finally yielding to this aesthetic adjuration, however, Dr. Yeats was to seek objectivity for the last time—in the drama.

III.

IN or about the commencement of the present century, over the old-fashioned premises then occupied by Morrow's Library, and now the property of Messrs. Hodges Figgis, the book-sellers, was to be found a more than usually depressing establishment known as The Nassau Hotel, approached by a flight of stairs, in almost complete darkness even at midday. This house of hospitality and entertainment has gone down before the growing demand for colour and light, even in matters of passing public accommodation: by a curious coincidence some of its rooms are now occupied by the Theosophical Society, thus forging a link with a former frequent client. Anyone possessed of common powers of observation passing the corner of South Frederick

Street in those now alarmingly distant days, must have been impressed by the continual entrances and exits upon the part of a tall young man, dressed in a black velvet jacket, with a more than usually profuse artist's bow, scuttling rapidly, his somewhat shortened arms clasped awkwardly behind his back, and muttering to himself as he stumbled along the neighbouring streets. This was William Butler Yeats, returned from London, from the friendship and influence of William Morris, as from the congenial association of the Rhymers' Club and the Cheshire Cheese, to his native Ireland of the Welcomes— God save the mark—to undertake no less a task than the foundation of a National Drama. More than one excellent and exhaustive book has been devoted to a critical examination and summary of this movement—a movement, incidentally, judged by its present-day results at all events, of greatly overrated importance in my private opinion : and I do not propose to do more than consider it from the standpoint of Dr. Yeats's personal contribution.

In 1899, Dr. Yeats had written : " We must make a theatre for ourselves and our friends, and for a few simple people who understand from sheer simplicity what we understand from scholarship and thought." Admirable words, animated by a surely justifiable hope ; has not another very different writer in our day stressed the fact that subtle and simple, Magi and shepherds united in

34

recognition of the revelation at Bethlehem? And again in the same Essay, subsequently included in *Ideas of Good and Evil:* " That the right people may escape the stupefying memory of the theatre of commerce, which clings even to them, our plays will be, for the most part, remote, spiritual, and ideal." Dr. Yeats's faith in even a limited public is touching, more especially in contrast to his subsequent disillusion upon this point of drama. A little further we read : " The theatre of commerce, the masterpiece of that movement towards externality in life and thought and art, against which the criticism of our day is learning to protest." The heel of Achilles is displayed at the outset, in this deprecation of objectivity, this proposed substitution of subjectivity upon the stage. A couple of years later Dr. Yeats wrote in *Samhain*, the periodical Bulletin of the National dramatic movement : " I hope to get our heroic age into verse, and to solve . . . . some problems of the speaking of verse to musical notes." Hope and courage of such high quality demand our praise, particularly when we recollect that the dramatist's contemplated public, however limited, had for the most part been catered for hitherto by such simple objective sentimental playwrights as Boucicault, who, as Dr. Yeats hastens to remind us a little later, " had no relation to literature." He has, also, in the course of the same periodical remarked that it is not possible to entirely and accurately foresee the ultimate

35

outcome of any particular artistic movement : and this observation is fully justified by the general scope and trend of the contemporary Abbey Theatre. A quarter of a century ago, a devoted band of a few dozen disciples, in the face of inadequate heating and other animal comforts, patiently attended *The Shadowy Waters*, followed by *The Shadow of the Glen*, separated by an interminable interval rendered still more penumbrous than the plays themselves by the wistful wailing of truly traditional Irish airs upon the violin, wielded by the impassive spectral figure of the late Dr. Arthur Darley. To-day the buffooneries of *Professor Tim* alternating with the " two-pence coloured " melodrama of *Juno and the Paycock*, can be counted upon to fill the house to capacity with a chocolate-consuming audience, who, presumably from weekly familiarity, anticipate each succeeding joke with indiscriminate and immoderate laughter, which results, perhaps mercifully, in rendering the ensuing joke inaudible; whose crescendo chatter during the intervals drowns even the most strenuous chords of Wagner or Beethoven; and who have, to their lasting discredit, insulted Dr. Larchet's delicate talent as a pianoforte executant. One turns, with not unreasonable relief, as no doubt does Dr. Yeats himself, from the contemplation of this theatrical Frankenstein, to a consideration of those far-off commencements, fraught with so many elusive, and alas ! unfulfilled

36

possibilities; and again, in the face of precise
and detailed volumes dealing with the movement,
I propose to be neither chronological nor comprehensive, but merely discursive and confined to
Dr. Yeats.

I can clearly recollect my first attendance at
an early, if not actual initial production of *On
Baile's Strand:* I remember vividly the admirable,
simple setting: the suggestion of sun and sea-
mist so wonderfully implied by a blue-green back-
cloth; the distant drone of waves upon a pebbly
beach, conveyed by some simple mechanical con-
trivance in the wings: and above all the exquisite
lyricism of many passages:

" *With that high laughing, turbulent head of hers
Thrown backward, and the bow-string at her
ear,
Or sitting at the fire, with those grave eyes
Full of good counsel, as it were with wine,
Or when love ran through all the lineaments
Of her wild body . . . .*"

Or, again:

" *The head grows prouder in the light of the
dawn,
And friendship thickens in the murmuring dark
Where the spare hazels meet the wool-white
foam.*"

But at no moment could I claim to have experi-
enced that emotion so aptly described by the
author himself: " So it is," he writes, " that in
the supreme moment of tragic art there comes
upon one that strange sensation as though the

37

hair of one's head stood up." The intellect was stirred, rather than the heart, which remained obstinately unwrung. There was, to hark back to the first definition of tragedy, to which Dr. Yeats himself has repeatedly subscribed, no purification even of the intellect by pity or by terror. This, at moments, exquisite essay in rhythm, gesture, and decoration, contained no such gross horror as when Lady Macbeth, fresh from the murder of Duncan, looking upon her hands, exclaims: " Who would have thought the old man to have had so much blood in him !" Nor did one hear any voice of lamentation comparable in intensity and simplicity to the cry of Lear over the body of Cordelia: " She's gone for ever !"

This peculiar deficiency in emotional content, this intellectual hardness, present to a greater or less extent in all Dr. Yeats's verse plays is not easy to explain. In the case of *On Baile's Strand* it certainly cannot be held to be due to the subject chosen: for next to Oedipus, there is possibly no situation more potentially tragic than the unwitting slaying of a son by his father: as a proof of this contention I may point out that Matthew Arnold, at whom Dr. Yeats has shown an inclination to tilt as a somewhat formal poet, in *Sohrab and Rustum*, based upon a similar legend of Persian origin, does succeed, with all his formality, in stirring the reader very deeply. Even Swinburne, whose rhetoric Dr. Yeats considers unforgivable

38

—and that Swinburne is frequently rhetorical no dispassionate critic will deny—nevertheless, even he, in that over-lyrical, obviously unactable, never-to-be-acted tragedy *Atalanta in Calydon*, in the outcries of Atalanta over the body of her son Meleager, whom she has been consciously instrumental in killing, stirs us to the depths with the tears of things:

> . . . " *O child,*
> *Son, first-born, fairest—O sweet mouth, sweet*
> *eyes,*
> *That drew my life out through my suckling*
> *breast,*
> *That shone and clove mine heart through—Oh*
> *soft knees*
> *Clinging, oh tender treadings of soft feet,*
> *Cheeks warm with little kissings—O child,*
> *child,*
> *What have we made each other?*
>
> *From this time*
> *Though mine eyes read to the end of all these*
> *things*
> *My lips shall not unfasten till I die.*"

I pass to the consideration of *Deirdre*, a later play, written about the meridian of Dr. Yeats's dramatic activity; and here again, despite the histrionic technique of Mrs. Patrick Campbell so generously employed, I was conscious of an element of emotional sterility. Beautiful as were the metaphors, tho' never so haunting the exquisite lyrics of the musicians, I could not, nor can I at many subsequent productions conscientiously sat

39

out in the hope of revising my opinion, sincerely sympathise with either Naoise or Deirdre. But in this play one comes upon a more vital objection: it contains an element of definite dramatic improbability, making full allowance always for poetic license. Deirdre, it may be remembered, snatches a knife from the musician, to hide it in her clothes; she begs of Conchubar permission to retire and perform the last rites of human decency upon the body of Naoise; and Conchubar replies, not altogether unintelligently:

" How do I know that you have not some knife,
And go to die upon his body?"

Deirdre counters, precisely as a woman would:

" Have me searched,
If you would make so little of your queen.
It may be that I have a knife hid here
Under my dress. Bid one of these dark slaves
To search me for it."

Conchubar concludes, after a stage direction of *Pause:*

" Go to your farewells, Queen."

Now the psychology of Conchubar in being unwilling to submit Deirdre to the indignity of a physical search by hired servants is entirely accurate and sound: but with his suspicions so roused, and so close upon the truth, certainly his consent to her withdrawal alone behind the curtain is unconvincing. Moreover, when the

40

curtains are subsequently drawn back, exhibiting
the practically foreseen suicide of Deirdre, his
expression of astonishment, seeing that, to all
intents and purposes, he himself, in common with
the audience, was almost in the secret from the
first, partakes of the nature of a flat anti-climax :

" No, no; I'll not believe it.   She is not dead—
She cannot have escaped a second time!"

To revert for a moment to *On Baile's Strand*, the
same straining of probability occurs : Cuchulain
gets so near the truth as to the young man's
identity, on the grounds of country, characteristics and personality, that we cannot feel as
intensely as we would wish that Fate and facts
have conspired to destroy him.

Perhaps the greatest tribute to Shakespeare, the
strongest proof that he may fairly be considered
the father of English poetic drama consists in
the enormous influence he has exerted upon
posterity : an influence which even Dr. Yeats, for
all his passionate search for literary individuality,
has been unable to altogether escape : an influence,
which likewise has not always been attended with
happiest results. Shakespeare upon several occasions has employed the introduction of humour
into his tragedies, presumably for purposes of
contrast; the most typical example of this device
is to be found in the drunken porter of *Macbeth*.
Personally, I find the entrance of this egregious
individual to partake of the nature of an excres-

41

cence; and in the case of Dr. Yeats, I regard a similar artifice as hardly to be borne. *Deirdre* is fortunately free from these mountebanks, as is also *The Countess Cathleen*, that exquisite piece of lyrical decorative tapestry whose slow unrolling formed the first production of the new-born Irish dramatic movement, and incidentally led to an acrimonious agitation in the press and elsewhere, thereby loading the dice at the outset against Dr. Yeats's project. But in *On Baile's Strand*, in the persons of The Blind Man and the Fool, we find lineal and presumably legitimate descendants of that drunken porter; and while freely admitting that it may be of the nature of an aesthetic deficiency in myself, nevertheless I have always wished their histrionic services might be dispensed with. I venture to apply the same criticism to *The King's Threshold*, which otherwise I would rank as one of the most complete and coherent of the verse plays: the Lord Mayor with his attendant cripples always impress me, not in the light of an artistic contrast, but rather an actual impediment to the essentially lyrical movement of the play. In Stephen Phillips's *Paolo and Francesca*, for example, in Dr. Yeats's own *Four Plays for Dancers*, the salt of humour has been omitted from the dish; yet these plays carry an emotional, if not a dramatic conviction to our palate to which *On Baile's Strand* and *The King's Threshold* cannot pretend. I believe that the introduction of this element of buffoonery may

42

have a subconscious origin in Dr. Yeats's attempt
to overcome an innate and progressive *subjectivity:*
to stiffen, as it were, the texture of his plays, by
coming to terms with the rough and tumble of
everyday life. The motive is assuredly worthy,
but the outcome, as is all too frequently the case
even with the most disinterested of motives, not
entirely happy. The supreme instance of this effort
to make his art more serviceable to the everyday
man in the street is to be found in the so-called
acting version of *The Shadowy Waters*, where he
attempts to substitute roystering Elizabethan able-
bodied men before the mast for those former pale,
semi-phantom figures which lend to the earlier
version a glamour comparable only to that of
Coleridge's *Ancient Mariner*. *The Shadowy
Waters* can hardly be regarded as a play at all—
not even a poetic play : it is intensely subjective :
nevertheless it is a type in itself—and not comparable to any other dramatic work I can recall :
and hence its relative, if limited and esoteric
success. *The King's Threshold* carries weight,
presumably because of the similarity between
Seanchan's intellectual position and that of Dr.
Yeats; presumably, further, because its tragic
action is largely confined to the sphere of intellect ;
and lastly, *The Countess Cathleen* fully justifies
itself as a thing of beauty and a joy for ever,
being concerned with a *subjective* spiritual conflict,
an abstract type of woman who, even in her
relations with Aleel, her poet lover, never comes

43

to terms with actual life at all. I venture to
suggest, then, that Dr. Yeats's comparative failure
as a poetic dramatist is due to the constant
presence of that subjective leaven in his material :
and to cause my inference to have less the appearance of impertinence I quote from that early
dedicatory letter to " A. E.," prefixed to *The
Secret Rose*. " I, on the other hand, believe that
poetry and romance cannot be made by the most
conscientious study of famous moments and of
the thoughts and feelings of *others*, but only by
looking into that little, infinite, faltering eternal
flame that one calls *oneself*." And again in the
preface to the volume entitled *Plays for an Irish
Theatre* I find superabundant proofs to sustain
my argument. " When we go back a few centuries,
and enter the great periods of drama," writes
Dr. Yeats, " character grows less and less, and
sometimes disappears, and there is much lyric
feeling, and at times a lyric measure will be
wrought into the dialogue . . . . in mainly tragic
art . . . . if the real world is not altogether rejected
it is but touched here and there, and into the
places we have left empty we summon rhythm,
balance, pattern, images . . . . all the chimeras
that haunt the edge of trance . . . . But alas ! it
is often my own words that break the dream . . . .
I discover that my language must keep at all
times a certain even richness." One has but to
place a passage where the poet is faithful to these
promptings of artistic conscience beside one where

44

he foregoes their influence, to realise the declension in value. Contrast, for example, Deirdre's outcry to the musicians in face of almost certain coming death :

" *Oh, singing women, set it down in a book*
That love is all we need, even though it is
But the last drops we gather up like this;
And though the drops are all we have known
  of life,
For we have been most friendless—praise us
  for it
And praise the double sunset, for naught's
  lacking,
But a good end to the long cloudy day."

Contrast this beauty with her outcry to Fergus :

    " *You never would return;*
I'll never look upon your face again.
Oh, keep him, Fergus; do not let him go,
But hold him from it. You are both wise and
  kind."

The conscious or unconscious sacrifice of *lyricism* in the last passage, renders it positively bald. Once more, when one reads the words of Forgael, in *The Shadowy Waters,*

" *We have fallen in the dreams the ever-living*
Breathe on the burnished mirror of the world,
And then smooth out with ivory hands and
  sigh,
And find their laughter sweeter to the taste
For that brief sighing,"

one is not prepared to find the same impalpable

45

creature of poetic fantasy, declare, a few pages
further:

> "*I cannot—I am going on to the end.*
>   *As for this woman, I think she is coming with*
>   *me.*"

One looks in vain in passages like these for that
" certain even richness " which Dr. Yeats almost
invariably seeks so patiently; but one can empha-
tically endorse with regretful surprise: " Alas,
it is my own words which break the dream !"
   There is yet a further point to which I would
venture to draw attention: it is the enormous
amount of patient and elaborate writing *concerning* the drama which Dr. Yeats has undertaken;
a bulk of literary work containing examples of
his best prose style. The wits will have it that
Mr. George Bernard Shaw's prefaces to his plays
are, at least in the reading, better than the plays
themselves; and in a similar spirit I have been
tempted at moments to prefer Dr. Yeats's stimu-
lating and suggestive views upon the theatre to
some at least of his dramatic work. All criticism
is inadequate, being of necessity limited and
personal, depending as much upon the mind and
temperament, the receptive capacity of the critic
as upon the essential qualities of the work considered; and this handicap is increased as I have
suggested, in dealing with strictly contemporary
work, for which one lacks the necessary perspective. Accepting these limitations, then, I cannot,

personally, disabuse myself of the suspicion that Dr. Yeats may be too much of a *dramatic theorist* to ever become an entirely successful *dramatist:* technique always tends to take precedence of inspiration. Moreover, these observations may at least claim to be reasonably consistent, even if founded upon false premises; for is not a theorist, in any department, of his very essence, subjective rather than objective? *The Countess Cathleen, The Land of Heart's Desire, The Hour Glass* and *The King's Threshold*, together with *The Shadowy Waters* represent, I think, plays where the author wrote with a certain subjectivity: I do not think they play very well upon the stage: it is difficult for them—to use the slang phrase— to get across. But I personally find a certain esoteric satisfaction in them, which is missing from those others where the poet possibly struggles to be something slightly different from himself. Moreover, if one contrasts *On Baile's Strand*, which treats of the Cuchulain legend in a simple objective fashion, with *At the Hawk's Well*, and *The Only Jealousy of Emer* from *Four Plays for Dancers*—which are concerned with the same cycle, but written from a subjective standpoint altogether personal and peculiar to Dr. Yeats—one cannot but admit the immeasurable artistic superiority of the latter creations; while the employment of ancient Irish epic legend as a foundation upon which to raise a superstructure of oriental mysticism provides a unique example of pouring

47

old wine into new bottles, if one may be permitted upon this solitary occasion to clumsily mix one's metaphors. Certainly, I am persuaded that Dr. Yeats found the poetic drama, in the conventional sense of the term, an inadequate vehicle of self-expression.

IV.

THE function of criticism is not incompatible with the practice of surmise: criticism deals largely with facts, and has not a fact been defined as a convergence of probabilities, and are not probabilities matters for permissible surmise? The new voice, startling and unexpected, with which Dr. Yeats spoke in *Responsibilities* for the first time, and with which he has continued to speak almost uninterruptedly since, came as a surprise to all, and as a shock to many of his admirers; and surmise, flavoured with a spice of gossip has been busy almost ever since. The publication of this book I regard as of cardinal importance. Many, who had hitherto followed the poet at first with admiration, then with doubt, not to say suspicion, now became permanently alienated. In a word, *Responsibilities* represents Dr. Yeats's final, irrevocable break with the sentimentalists, literary and political: it has narrowed, but, if one may say so, intensified his public; and out of an unrestrained subjectivity based largely upon memory, sole surviving parent

48

apparently of Art—this new method has enriched English letters, whatever views are held of Irish, with individualistic love-poetry and satire, for which I personally can find a parallel only in the work of Donne. The more personal causes of this artistic " bouleversement "— surely almost unique in literature—must, until all available facts are laid open to posterity, providing an enlightened posterity with that necessary perspective to which I have more than once alluded, remain speculative. Hence, in the following remarks, a forbearing reader will understand that I merely advance for his consideration my own personal opinions.

The Countess Cathleen, with which the National Dramatic movement was virtually launched, drew fire from the extreme wing of orthodox, or dare one say, superficial commonplace thought. *Cathleen Ni Houlihan* notwithstanding, the subsequent verse plays did not prove entirely congenial to the provincial sentimentalists so suitably catered for by Boucicault and Co., whose artistic qualifications Dr. Yeats had shown the temerity to question. Moreover, his fellow-dramatists were not held entirely free from offence: Synge had shown, in spite of *Riders to the Sea*, which every sentimentalist who ran might read, a tendency to take liberty with the Boucicault convention; but public opinion was hardly sufficiently prepared for the shock of *The Playboy of the Western World.* A due considera-tion of this storm in a theatrical tea-cup belongs to the criticism of Synge and not of Yeats: but mention of it I consider unavoidable and most pertinent. I was personally present at the production of *The Playboy*—and at the subsequent open discussion: I am not likely to forget the display of violence and intimidation upon this and following occasions: and while I am not competent to assess the precise value of their effect upon the author of the play, I do consider that they must have considerably shaken Dr. Yeats, in showing him clearly for the first time, a section of that public with whom he had undertaken to deal. Whether Dr. Yeats's estimate of Synge's work was an overrated one, is another point extraneous to my present scope: the fact remains that his estimate was exalted: and the repudiation, expressed in almost brutal terms, may well have impressed Synge's literary sponsor in the light of practically a personal assault: and personal assaults, particularly when one believes them unmerited, have a disturbing effect.

The quarrel between Synge and the public gradually expanded to include his fellow dramatists: a stage was eventually reached at which the point at issue involved the national value or otherwise of any and every variety of artistic activity: and just when the controversy showed signs of dying down before more pressing political distractions, Sir Hugh Lane offered his pictures to the Irish Nation, coupled with the proposal for an Art Gallery to be designed by

Sir Edward Lutyens. It is more than possible that, dispassionately considered, there was something to be said upon both sides in the dispute over *The Playboy;* but no shred of justification can be held to exist for the treatment Sir Hugh Lane received at the hands of an ignorant lower middle class and proletariat. A section of the public press condescended to methods of the most unscrupulous nature: one evening journal publishing what purported to be the architect's design— in reality an exquisite conception—representing a structure hideous, inadmissible, and impossible: while specially convened sittings of our whilom City Fathers lashed themselves into fury, somewhat inconsequently directed against Lady Gregory, unfortunate, or rather fortunate, perhaps, in possessing an intimate relationship to the donor of the proposed pictures. In this particular case the dust of the conflict settled earlier than usual: the eyes of our city fathers, and of the public whom they have the privilege to adequately represent, are in consequence cleared: most, but unfortunately not all, of Sir Hugh Lane's pictures are to-day housed in a gallery not entirely inadequate, containing, in addition, a bust of the donor, who has mercifully passed— if one may quote in such a modern connexion the phrase of a Victorian poet—to where beyond these voices there is peace: and who, among Elysian fields, more delightful as one may wish than the most delightful pastoral creations of his

51

beloved French impressionists, may console himself with the knowledge of a double debt under which he has laid the citizens of our city—the gift of his pictures—and the provocation to Dr. Yeats which resulted in certain poems from *Responsibilities*.

I have reserved the most intimate, the most personal factor for the last, although first in point of consideration and quotation: "cherchez la femme," cry our French cousins in their slang phrase, not very wide of the mark upon most occasions. The later poetry of Yeats is overshadowed by a cloud of intensely personal passion: the point of consuming interest for the critic is—the sincerity or otherwise of this passion. The question of sincerity in the generally accepted sense of the word, is not, perhaps, quite as easily disposed of as one might at first sight believe; for in coming to a decision one is hampered by much that the poet has written concerning the antithetical self—the capacity to assume one of a certain few tragic poses before one can fully express oneself as an artist. Into the complexity of the esoteric doctrine of the mask and antithetical self, so dwelt upon by Dr. Yeats of recent years, I do not propose to enter at the moment: but taking the term *tragic pose* at its face value in current English, I have to envisage a possible insincerity in those so admirable later love poems contained in *Responsibilities*, and subsequent volumes. I am prepared to envisage insincerity, but not to too seriously contemplate it—for I cannot believe that so intensely personal and convincing an art could ever have root in anything but reality of experience. At all events, I would suggest that in Dr. Yeats's case, a rising subjective tension, due to a variety of causes, had attained that precise point at which, granted the faculty of adequate expression, truly personal poetry is possible. Physicists have demonstrated how a solution of any particular chemical, upon reaching a certain degree of saturation, will suddenly undergo visible precipitation in definite crystalline form upon slight mechanical stimulus; some analogous emotional process may be held to account for verse possessing the unique, bitter-sweet savour, the austere, almost harsh outlines exhibited by *No Second Troy*.

" *Why should I blame her that she filled my days*
With misery, or that she would of late
Have taught to ignorant men most violent ways,
Or hurled the little streets upon the great,
Had they but courage equal to desire?
What could have made her peaceful with a
  mind
That nobleness made simple as a fire,
With beauty like a tightened bow, a kind
That is not natural in an age like this,
Being high and solitary and most stern?
Why, what could she have done being what
  she is?
Was there another Troy for her to burn?"

Again, in *A Thought from Propertius*, the poet shows that he had not learned drawing at the

53

Art School entirely in vain, when immature and undecided as to a career:

> " *She might, so noble from head*
> *To great shapely knees*
> *The long flowing line,*
> *Have walked to the altar*
> *Through the holy images*
> *At Pallas Athene's side*
> *Or been fit spoil for a centaur*
> *Drunk with the unmixed wine.*"

While that peculiar capacity of our people to embody their semi-mystical aspirations in a human personification reverberates through the pathos of *Fallen Majesty:*

> " *Although crowds gathered once if she but*
> *   showed her face,*
> *And even old men's eyes grew dim, this hand*
> *   alone,*
> *Like some lost courtier at a gipsy camping place,*
> *Babbling of fallen majesty, records what's*
> *   gone.*
>
> *The lineaments, a heart that laughter has made*
> *   sweet,*
> *These, these remain, but I record what's gone.*
> *A crowd*
> *Will gather, and not know it walks the very*
> *   street*
> *Whereon a thing once walked that seemed a*
> *   burning cloud.*"

The celebration of children in poetry forms no inconsiderable province of the domain of English verse: much of such literature might be held

54

suspect of sentimentality; it has remained for Dr. Yeats to discover a new, an intellectual, line of approach to childhood, and to project it in his art. Moreover, the various factors responsible for his recent temperamental eruption meet and fuse in the brief exquisite lines entitled, *To a Child Dancing in the Wind:*

> " *Dance there upon the shore;*
> *What need have you to care*
> *For wind or water's roar?*
> *And tumble out your hair*
> *That the salt drops have wet;*
> *Being young you have not known*
> *The fool's triumph, nor yet*
> *Love lost as soon as won,*
> *Nor the best labourer dead*
> *And all the sheaves to bind.*
> *What need have you to dread*
> *The monstrous crying of wind?*"

Two years later the poet speaks to the child again :

> " *Has no one said those daring*
> *Kind eyes should be more learn'd?*
> *Or warned you how despairing*
> *The moths are when they are burned,*
> *I could have warned you, but you are young,*
> *So we speak a different tongue.*
>
> *Oh, you will take whatever's offered*
> *And dream that all the world's a friend,*
> *Suffer as your mother suffered,*
> *Be as broken in the end.*
> *But I am old and you are young,*
> *And I speak a barbarous tongue.*"

55

I have alluded, at the outset, to Dr. Yeats's consistency—that his later work is in basic essentials the logical outcome or superstructure of his earlier: I have furthermore drawn attention to the purification of his artistic manner from luxuriance and irrelevancy; I feel impelled to substantiate this latter argument once again by placing side by side an early love poem with a later. Many years previous the poet had written under the title *A Poet to His Beloved:*

"*I bring you with reverent hands*
The books of my numberless dreams;
White woman that passion has worn
As the tide wears the dove-grey sands,
And with heart more old than the horn
That is brimmed from the pale fire of time:
White woman with numberless dreams
I bring you my passionate rhyme."

In *The Wild Swans at Coole*, under the simple title *Memory*, he treats once more of love in his newly discovered manner:

"*One had a lovely face,*
And two or three had charm,
But charm and face were in vain
Because the mountain grass
Cannot but keep the form
Where the mountain hare has lain."

For beauty, linked with austerity and precision, I can find no parallel for these six short lines but in the Greek Anthology: while for their possession I should be tempted to forego more than one *Lake Isle of Innisfree.*

One detects, as I have suggested, in the lines
To a Child Dancing in the Wind some reference
to those other factors in the production of Dr.
Yeats's disillusion and discontent, and to which
more explicit allusion is made in certain poems; in
that entitled *To a Wealthy Man*, and also in the
lines *To a Shade*, that bitter apostrophe to Parnell
containing the dry-point etching of twilit Dublin.

> " *When the day is spent,*
> *To drink of that salt breath out of the sea*
> *When grey gulls flit about instead of men,*
> *And the gaunt houses put on majesty.*"

In the case of *To a Wealthy Man* the quarrel over
Sir Hugh Lane's proposed gift undergoes a
process of sublimation for which the poet shows
a capacity almost unique in contemporary letters;
as a result, Dr. Yeats does a greater service to the
Dublin of his day by a truly *saeva indignatio*,
comparable to that of Swift, than could the most
sentimental eulogist: in the domain of passion
our city has become comparable to Troy; while
in the sphere of art a parallel is to be found in
the Cities of Renaissance Italy. Even while he
scourges us, the poet shows us that destiny he
believes to be our due:

> " *Look up in the sun's eye and give*
> *What the exultant heart calls good*
> *That some new day may breed the best*
> *Because you gave, not what they would,*
> *But the right twigs for an eagle's nest!*"

57

Nevertheless, disenchantment extends even to his own work, dramatic and lyrical:

> " There's something ails our colt
> That must, as if it had not holy blood,
> Nor on Olympus leaped from cloud to cloud,
> Shiver under the lash, strain, sweat and jolt
> As though it dragged road metal. My curse
>   on plays
> That have to be set up in fifty ways,
> On the day's war with every knave and dolt,
> Theatre business, management of men."

In the extremity of his acrimony he repudiates his early poetry in an ejaculation of classical precision and pungency against his numerous imitators:

> " I made my song a coat
>   Covered with embroideries
>   Out of old mythologies
>   From heel to throat;
> But the fools caught it,
>   Wore it in the world's eyes
> As though they'd wrought it.
>   Song, let them take it,
> For there's more enterprise
>   In walking naked."

And upon this advice his Muse has acted henceforth, giving to all his later work that peculiar intellectual hardness, that austerity of emotion, and exquisite economy of phrase, so violent a contrast to his earlier style, which nevertheless has for me, at all events, so enduring and so severe a charm.

But these quarrelsome preoccupations bulk relatively small in comparison with his " grand passion " to which he inevitably returns, with progressively less bitterness and more of pathos :

" *I had this thought a while ago,*
 ' My darling cannot understand
What I have done, or what would do
In this blind, bitter land . . . .'

That every year I have cried, ' At length
My darling understands it all,
Because I have come into my strength,
And words obey my call.'

That had she done so who can say
What would have shaken from the sieve?
I might have thrown poor words away
And been content to live."

The last verse quoted from this poem, *The Consolation* with an implied hope of escape from his own increasing subjectivity into an objective world under the influence of consummated love, impresses me with an obscure and painful poignancy, enhanced by the last two lines from *Reconciliation:*

" *But dear, cling close to me: since you were*
 gone,
 My barren thoughts have chilled me to the
 bone."

" Hope and Memory," he had written many years ago, " have one daughter, and her name is Art. Oh, beloved daughter of Hope and Memory be with me for a little !" Art has remained with

59

him, although, in the absence of one parent she has come to lean more and more upon the breast of Memory; and upon that breast she becomes less passionate, less importunate, like a tired child at evening; and out of this mood of regretful reverie suddenly arises the exquisite serene retrospect of the lines entitled *The Wild Swans at Coole:*

" *The trees are in their autumn beauty,*
The woodland paths are dry,
Under the October twilight the water
Mirrors a still sky;
Upon the brimming water among the stones
Are nine-and-fifty swans . . . .

I have looked upon those brilliant creatures,
And now my heart is sore.
All's changed since I, hearing at twilight,
The first time on this shore,
The bell-beat of their wings above my head,
Trod with a lighter tread . . . .

But now they drift on the still water
Mysterious, beautiful;
Among what rushes will they build,
By what lake's edge or pool
Delight men's eyes when I awake some day
To find they have flown away?"

The poet, through many tribulations, has entered upon his kingdom. I can find no fitting parallel for the last verse of this poem other than Keats's *Ode on a Grecian Urn;* both exhibit the passionate desire to fix for eternity the essentially fugitive beauty of a moment; while out of this retrospective reverie arises the best, the most personal, and by a logical necessity, the most subjective of the later poems. Dr. Yeats had, about this time, and subsequent to his marriage, settled in the ancient tower of Thoor Ballylee, whose feudal atmosphere also influences the work of this autumnal period; *In Memory of Major Robert Gregory* enumerates those friends whom he would wish to have entertained at his house-warming:

" *All, all are in my thoughts to-night, being dead*
   . . . .
  But not a friend that I would bring
  This night can set us quarrelling,
  For all that come into my mind are dead."

Lionel Johnson, John Synge, George Pollexfen, Robert Gregory:

" *I had thought, seeing how bitter is that wind*
  That shakes the shutter, to have brought to
    mind
  All those that manhood tried, or childhood
    loved
  Or boyish intellect approved." . . . .

That bitter wind upon the shutter is not long silent henceforth in the work of Yeats, conveying a peculiar cold melancholy not present in any other poet. His isolation, intellectual, even physical, appears embodied in the very structure of that stark building which entitles one of the most valuable volumes of his later verse:

61

> " I turn away and shut the door, and on the stair
>   Wonder how many times I could have proved
>   my worth
>   In something that all others understand or
>   share;
>   But oh, ambitious heart, had such a proof drawn
>   forth
>   A company of friends, a conscience set at ease,
>   It had but made us pine the more."

Had not the poet already commended his former companions of the Cheshire Cheese inasmuch as they were of those who

> " never made a poorer song
>   That you might have a heavier purse,
>   Nor gave loud service to a cause
>   That you might have a troop of friends "?

Had he come to regard the price of intellectual independence as too heavy? A price heavier in Ireland possibly than anywhere else; where, in the tumult upon *The Playboy*, he had already discovered the strength of the herd instinct, yet had nevertheless hoped so passionately, as he declared at the time in public, that " the generation of young men and girls who are now leaving schools or colleges are weary of the tyranny of clubs and leagues. They wish again for individual sincerity, the eternal quest for truth, all that has been given up for so long that all might crouch upon the one roost, or cry and quack in the one flock."

I think it permissible to suppose that in most

62

cases children, being objective projections of our personality, provide a partial solution of that complex in which every introverted character finds itself at moments in its relation with the world. But in Dr. Yeats's case his two children appear to serve but as fresh material for subjective self-torment:

> " *And yet it seems*
> *Life scarce can cast a fragrance on the wind,*
> *Scarce spread a glory to the morning beams,*
> *But the torn petals strew the garden plot;*
> *And there's but common greenness after that.*
>
> *And what if my descendants lose the flower*
> *Through natural declension of the soul,*
> *Through too much business with the passing*
> *   hour,*
> *Through too much play, or marriage with a*
> *   fool?*
> *May this laborious stair and this stark tower*
> *Become a roofless ruin that the owl*
> *May build in the cracked masonry and cry*
> *Her desolation to the desolate sky.*"

I personally feel that the decent limits of bitterness are reached in many of these poems; I am driven to forego my own conviction already stated, and to prefer the possibility in certain cases, at all events, of a tragic pose: I am impelled to quote against their author the last verse from *The Stare's Nest by my Window*, with its passionate solicitude for at least a little sweetness, however ephemeral:

63

" My wall is loosening; honey-bees
Come build in the empty house of the stare . . .
We had fed the heart on fantasies,
The heart's grown brutal from the fare . . . .
                                    Oh, honey bees
Come build in the empty house of the stare."

Close upon a quarter of a century ago Dr. Yeats
had written in the first flush of enthusiasm that
the literary cry in Ireland was then the same as
it had been a little earlier in Russia: the cry "to
the people." Hence *Cathleen Ni Houlihan*, hence
a theatre where many would understand from sheer
simplicity what the poets and dramatists understood from subtlety. Christianity and the old
nature faith had lain down side by side in the
cottages, exclaimed Dr. Yeats, and he would
proclaim that marriage as loudly as possible.
Upon the creepy stool beside the fire was alone
to be found that imaginative life which had
become debilitated if not moribund among the
so-called cultured classes. A democracy of culture
indeed, nothing less was this young man's vision;
all of which was scarcely consistent preface for
the exquisite arrogance of those lines from
Responsibilities, entitled *Upon a House Shaken
by the Land Agitation:*

" How should the world be luckier if this house,
Where passion and precision have been one
Time out of mind, became too ruinous
To breed the lidless eye that loves the sun?

64

> *. . . . Although*
> *Mean roof-trees were the sturdier for its fall,*
> *How should their luck run high enough to*
> * reach*
> *The gifts that govern man, and after these*
> *To gradual Time's last gift, a written speech*
> *Wrought of high laughter, loveliness and ease?"*

Nor was the reader sufficiently prepared for *These are the Clouds:*

> *" These are the clouds about the fallen sun,*
> *The majesty that shuts his burning eye;*
> *The weak lay hand on what the strong has done,*
> *Till that be tumbled that was lifted high*
> *And discord follow upon unison,*
> *And all things at one common level lie."*

Again, lest any generous doubt should remain in the reader's mind, the poet finally and further writes :

> *" All things can tempt me from this craft of*
> * verse:*
> *One time it was a woman's face, or worse—*
> *The seeming needs of my fool-driven land."*

To resolve this paradox was beyond the capacity of the average Irish reader perhaps; the apparent contradiction resulted, as I have said earlier, in Yeats's final irrevocable break with the sentimentalist who, as he declares, desires to deceive himself, and with the rhetorician, whose object is to attempt to deceive others. Now the sentimentalist and the rhetorician between them constitute no inconsiderable fraction of our national public; consequently the poet's adherents have diminished in number, but I venture to think, have gained in discrimination.

This substitution of the big house for the thatched cottage, has, moreover, produced some results from the literary standpoint at all events, whose charm no dispassionate reader may fairly deny:

" *Sound of a stick upon the floor, a sound*
From somebody that toils from chair to chair;
Beloved books that famous hands have bound,
Old marble heads, old pictures everywhere;
Great rooms where travelled men and children
*   found*
Content or joy; a last inheritor
Where none has reigned that lacked a name and
*   fame*
Or out of folly into folly came."

So is it written of Coole and Ballylee in the days of their fullness: turn now to the inevitable melancholy reverse of the Irish political and social medal:

" *Here, traveller, scholar, poet, take your stand*
When all those rooms and passages are gone,
When nettles wave upon a shapeless mound
And saplings root among the broken stone,
And dedicate—eyes bent upon the ground,
Back turned upon the brightness of the sun
And all the sensuality of the shade—
A moment's memory to that laurelled head."

I venture, at the risk of becoming wearisome, to indicate the poet's implication of subjectivity, his

deprecation of objectivity, in the attitude desired
for that future pilgrim; and I turn for a last
example of Dr. Yeats's disillusion—or dare I say
illumination?—to that poem from *The Winding
Stair, In Memory of Eva Gore-Booth* and *Con
Markievicz* :

> " *The light of evening, Lissadell,
>   Great windows open to the south.*"

I read no more, entranced by these two utterly
simple yet incomparable lines: for at their
evocation I stand again upon the scabious-covered
slopes of Bornasorge, high over Bo More, above
that lake where the starlings gather in the reeds;
I see Ben Bulben crouched upon the right, like
a leviathan, and to the north the crenellations of
the mountains of Donegal, culminating in Slieve
League flinging back the afterflush from his steep
face as the sun falls to the Atlantic: far out
upon the left, beyond Knocklane Hill, Roughley
stretches, a pointing finger out to sea: opposite
and sunk below, across the narrow silting channel
of Drumcliff, where the seals bask in the brief
midday sun, and where wailing sea-swallows nest
among windblown bent, I see Lissadell again, in
that light of evening, with its great windows
open to the south; and I hasten to take up the
book, and read again:

> " *Two girls in silk kimonos, both
>   Beautiful, one a gazelle.*"

I recollect those two girls, now dead. I recall

67

Eva Gore-Booth, *The Little Waves of Breffny:* I
remember Constance, the Citizen Army, " all that
delirium of the brave." I hear the voice of a
young, enthusiastic, trustful man declaiming his
passionate assurance that he shall find his heaven
where he first crept upon the floor : I hear the
same voice, less confident, declare, in middle age,
that he has walked once upon Sinbad's yellow
strand, and never may another hit his fancy;
for the last time, shaken by what another far
different poet has termed " sudden pity for the
poor torn past," I turn the page once more,
confident that I shall find here at last the fruit of
that long-desired marriage of Hope and Memory :

> *" Dear shadows, now you know it all,*
>   *All the folly of a fight*
>   *With a common wrong or right . . . ."*

Only that : nothing more. Can it be then, that
William Butler Yeats, Doctor of Literature, Vice-
President of the Irish Academy of Letters, Winner
of the Nobel Prize, one of the most striking,
courageous and independent personalities of my
time, comparable, in my opinion, to Parnell and
to Swift, is like Parnell and Swift, a planter in
outlook after all, and to the end ? Were not even
the Gore-Booths themselves, planters likewise at
least in origin : where is consolation to be found :
who is a true Irishman ? As to Nationality, one
possesses but the somewhat time-dried sop :
Hiberniores Hibernicis ipsis: while for consolation

68

in the matter of those gallant even if granted
misguided ladies of Lissadell, I turn, with that
ironic inconsequence which is of the very essence
of life, to *Responsibilities:*

" *They weighed so lightly what they gave,*
  But let them be, they're dead and gone,
  They're with O'Leary in the grave."

V.

THE prose writing of poets has, in most instances,
·suffered an undue neglect; there is a tendency,
possibly, to regard it somewhat in the light of
an inferior practice, not deserving of so much
serious consideration as their more proper function
of verse.   Thus, how many readers who have
studied and enjoyed the minor poems of Milton,
or even the *Paradise Lost*, can honestly claim an
equal degree of familiarity with the *Aeropagitica*
or *Tetrachordon?*   Yet Milton's style in prose is
surely of equal literary value as in his verse.
Again, certain poems of Thomas Gray may almost
be termed popular, from general familiarity; but
who reads Gray's excellent letters, conveying a
far more intimate sense of personality than any
of his poetry?   Shelley, as represented by *The
Cloud*, or *The Skylark*, or *The Ode to the West
Wind* has become the property of the college
classroom; few read *The Defence of Poetry*, or
The Letters from Abroad; while Keats's letters,

more particularly the later ones, admirable as they are, interest hardly any of those who can quote easily, say, from the great *Odes*. Contemporary with Dr. Yeats, we have the case of Lionel Johnson, whose chiselled verse formed the lesser bulk of that scholarly austere art: his *Post Liminium*, and *Art of Thomas Hardy*, representing, I think, the best criticism since Arnold or Walter Pater. Finally, Dr. Yeats as a prose writer has, as far as I am aware, never been adequately treated, or, at any length: his poetry having characteristically overshadowed the other branch of his work. Some, even among those acquainted with his writing, may learn with surprise that Dr. Yeats possesses a novel to his credit: let me rather say, a novelette, the diminutive being justified upon the score of length. I possess a copy of the second edition of this little book, published originally in *The Pseudonym Library* under the pen-name of " Ganconagh "; I regard it as of prime importance in connexion with the origins of Dr. Yeats's work; it shows that preoccupation with Sligo which characterises the early poetry of his objective period, and has for a central *motif* the homesickness of Sherman, temporarily exiled in London, in the employment of an uncle, whom I suspect of being a Pollexfen family portrait; in point of fact I am persuaded that John Sherman himself is but the projection upon paper of the youthful William Butler Yeats, resident, like Sherman, in Hammersmith, fretting for Sligo

70

town, thinly veiled under the name of **Ballah**. The autobiographical element, always implicit, becomes explicit upon one occasion which compels quotation :—

" The grey corner of a cloud slanting its rain upon Cheapside called to mind by some remote suggestion the clouds rushing and falling in cloven surf on the seaward steep of a mountain north of Ballah . . . . Delayed by a crush in the Strand, he heard a faint trickling of water near by; it came from a shop-window, where a little water-jet balanced a wooden ball upon its point. The sound suggested a cataract with a long Gaelic name, that leaped crying into the Gate of the Winds at Ballah . . . . He was set dreaming a whole day by walking down . . . . to the border of the Thames . . . . it made him remember an old day-dream of his . . . . a certain wood-bordered and islanded lake, whither in childhood he had often gone blackberry gathering. At the further end was a little island called Inniscrewin . . . . Often when life and its difficulties had seemed to him like the lessons of some elder boy given to a younger by mistake, it had seemed good to dream of going away to that islet and building a wooden hut there, and burning a few years out, rowing to and fro, fishing, or lying on the island slopes . . . . "

I venture to think that reasonable imaginative intuition would divine in this passage the emotional foundation of *The Lake Isle of Innisfree*, even in the absence of Dr. Yeats's

71

confirmation provided in *The Trembling of the Veil*, the autobiography of his adolescence:

> " I had still the ambition, formed in Sligo in my teens, of living in imitation of Thoreau on Innisfree, a little island in Lough Gill, and when walking through Fleet Street very home-sick I heard a little tinkle of water, and saw a fountain in a shop-window which balanced a little ball upon the jet, and began to remember lake water. From the sudden remembrance came my poem *Innisfree* . . . ."

The power to evoke Irish landscape, the capacity to produce *atmosphere* is also present in the germ in *John Sherman*, although this immature method is less elaborate, less deliberate, less sophisticated, one may say, than it subsequently became under the influence of literary self-consciousness.

> " The town was dripping, but the rain was almost over. The large drops fell seldomer and seldomer into the puddles. It was the hour of ducks . . . . The water slid noise-lessly, and one or two of the larger stars made little roadways of fire into the darkness . . . . once or twice a fish leaped. Along the banks were the vague shadows of houses, seeming like phantoms gathering to drink . . . ."

Those who are acquainted with Sligo, or any West of Ireland town upon a wet evening, must admit the adequacy of this representation, and also of a subsequent description:

" The women selling gooseberries; the
river bridge; the high walls of the garden
where it was said the gardener used to see
the ghost of a former owner in the shape
of a rabbit . . . . the deserted flour store;
the wharves covered with grass . . . . grey
clouds covering the town with flying shadows
rushed by like the old and dishevelled eagles
that Maeldune saw hurrying towards the
waters of life"

The most important quality, however, in this
tentative little excursion into fiction, properly so
called, consists in a degree of simplicity, of human
sympathy, of sentiment, not to say of sentimentality, which does not appear again in any
subsequent work. There is nothing abstract in
the group of characters, nothing, might one even
say, distinguished; yet although ordinary, the
author succeeds in making them essentially alive
and interesting: while the reflections upon everyday life which occasionally emerge, display a
practical acumen which one would not expect
from Dr. Yeats, merely upon a survey of his more
representative work. The mood which produced
John Sherman never returned; and the short tale
Dhoya included in the same little paper-covered
volume is in tune with the stories contained in
The Secret Rose.

I have already casually alluded to these stories
in dealing with his early poetry; and I repeat
once more, that together with *Stories of Red
Hanrahan*, they constitute for me, at all events,

73

the most delectable productions of this period.
I find in them the closest approach to a perfect
blend of the subjective and objective method,
usually divorced in Dr. Yeats's art. The setting
and background of Sligo scenery, while faithfully
evoked, are kept in artistic subordination; while
the mystical spirit, to use that much discredited
term, is relatively simple and direct, in sharp
refreshing contrast with the subsequent esoteric
complexity of the " antithetical self," and the
" phases of the moon." Thus *The Wisdom of the
King* deals symbolically with the inevitable
isolation of those whom the gods foredoom to
genius; *The Crucifixion of the Outcast* represents
that hostility with which systematised thought
invariably reacts to individual expression : while
The Heart of the Spring proclaims that in death
alone can the spirit attain to perfect initiation.
Possibly the most interesting is that entitled *The
Old Men of the Twilight*, in which the topography
of The Rosses and Rosses Point is carefully and
beautifully employed; moreover, the fate of the
old learned men, who were too preoccupied with
their academic dispute to listen to the words of
Patrick, and in consequence were changed into
herons, those most lonely birds, always impresses
me as having a certain personal application to the
author. It is, perhaps, a curious sequence that in
Calvary, the last and most metaphysical of *The
Four Plays for Dancers*, Dr. Yeats portrays a
solitary white heron as the type of extreme sub-

74

jectivity, one of those for whom he claims Christ died in vain; indeed, throughout these stories there runs that suggestion of a type of intellectual isolation "shuddering at its own consuming solitude."

The *Stories of Red Hanrahan* afford the supreme instance of that frequently unfortunate revision to which allusion has already been made. Under the influence, presumably, of the late Lady Gregory, Dr. Yeats undertook to re-write these exquisite sketches in " Kiltartanese " ; a procedure in futility and violence to the originals analogous to the transformation of the ship's crew of *The Shadowy Waters*. Only one justification exists for the change—namely, the creation of that additional episode where Hanrahan is offered the fourfold mystical gift by the ancient women of the Shee. Hanrahan is depicted as unequal to the occasion, and his life wilts and commences to drift from that moment, while Mary Lavelle, the human woman whom he has loved, is irrevocably lost to him. In the original version these stories rank with *The Secret Rose* for beauty and individuality of conception and execution. *The Vision of Hanrahan* excels in elusive delicacy. The wandering hedge poet has climbed the hill, and stands above the Glencar Valley, whose hollow is filled with vapour. He aimlessly casts the petals of a wild rose which he has plucked away upon the wind, and as he does so, a phantom troop arise out of the abyss. These are all the lovers of Irish

75

legend, culminating in Dermot and Dervorgilla who drift towards and speak to him; and as the vision fades away into the mist again before the terrified shriek of Hanrahan, " a little below the edge of the cliff the troop of petals still fluttered in the air, for the gateway of Eternity had opened and closed in a pulsation of the heart." It is my considered opinion, for what it is worth, that had Dr. Yeats written nothing more than *The Secret Rose* with *Stories of Red Hanrahan*, his position, even although a minor one, in the realm of Anglo-Irish letters was almost assured.

In spite of much obvious autobiography, *John Sherman* may fairly be considered objective in type, while the other stories considered hold a delicate balance between extroversion and introversion; but in *Rosa Alchemica, The Tables of the Law*, and *The Adoration of the Magi*, an entirely new element of metaphysical speculation is introduced, which has remained with Dr. Yeats to the present day as an abiding interest of profound importance to himself, he frequently assures us. I confess frankly that this is an aspect of the poet which appeals least to me personally. The individuals in these stories who dabble in Alchemy, while conversing in a jargon composed of a smattering of mystical theology mixed with decadence, impress me as approaching perilously to the " high-falutin "; their postures before tapestries embroidered with peacocks' feathers, their robing of themselves in long garments are

76

detailed in a style savouring distastefully of preciosity. *The Adoration of the Magi*, in the hands of a French writer such as Anatole France, might conceivably convince by measure of ingenious blasphemy. But the three frieze-coated individuals, waiting patiently in the house of ill-fame to write down a message which never really becomes clearly articulate for transcription have for me a faintly ridiculous suggestion. Dr. Yeats, in his writings about the theatre, ceaselessly inveighs against the artistic immorality of melodrama : *Rosa Alchemica*, *The Tables of the Law*, with *The Adoration of the Magi* are, I fear, to be held suspect of that crime. Above all, I resent them as the precursors of that trend of thought which has as its illogical conclusion The Mask, The Antithetical Self, and the Phases of the Moon; an abstract desert where poetry withers of necessity, leading me mournfully to quote the lines from *Lamia:*

> " *Doth not all charm fly*
> *At the mere touch of cold philosophy?*"

Every artist, being human, exhibits some temperamental or intellectual deficiency : some may consider Shakespeare as lacking in a sense of form, Milton as exalting form at the expense of emotion, Dante as sacrificing aesthetic beauty to an amateur interest in theology, and universal human interest to political acrimony. Having mentioned such a distinguished trilogy, I trust

77

that I may be held excused if I include Dr. Yeats also in this category of relative imperfection. I consider Dr. Yeats at moments one of the supreme literary artists of the day : but I also consider him to possess an imperfectly developed sense of humour. This handicap, apart from its obvious disability, operates further by causing Dr. Yeats to take indifferent matters seriously, and to attach undue importance to relatively trivial themes. Had Dr. Yeats's humorous faculty permitted a more extended self-criticism, I believe we might have been spared much of *Rosa Alchemica, The Tables of the Law*, and *The Adoration of the Magi;* and had his sense of intellectual proportion, a logical outcome of a sense of humour, functioned more actively, I do not think his many genuine admirers would have been subjected to the trivialities contained in *The Celtic Twilight.* Furthermore, I think it possible that the contents of this book tend to show that Dr. Yeats does not entirely comprehend the Irish " peasant," to use that presently discredited term. The people of the countryside are, or at all events were, a quarter of a century ago, polite : they are, or were, likewise, accommodating and anxious to please : and it would have gone hard indeed with them to defraud the youthful, enthusiastic, but indiscriminating collector of folklore of more than his due meed of pishogues, lepracauns, and banshees. I am willing to consent to the proposition that Dr. Yeats collected and printed these puerilities in good faith: which serves but to prove my contention that his sense of humour is imperfect. I hasten to close the pages of *The Celtic Twilight* in order to turn to the consideration of *Ideas of Good and Evil*, that collection of essays some of which perhaps are difficult to overpraise.

Some thirty years ago, or thereabout, began that general intellectual activity among us which a little later became known as *The Irish Literary Revival*. Subsequent dramatic events, chiefly of a political nature, displaced the movement from public interest, combining with certain inherent points of weakness to render it largely abortive; but, should interest in the period ever return, the future student will find no better exposition of the underlying motives than that provided by certain essays in *Ideas of Good and Evil*. I consider that in some of these papers Dr. Yeats has achieved the unique—which might almost appear impossible at first sight. He has given to frankly artistic propaganda an enduring literary form. *What is Popular Poetry? The Theatre*, and above all, *Ireland and the Arts*, should afford adequate justification for George Moore's pronouncement that " the whole Irish literary movement arose out of Yeats, and returns to Yeats." Moreover, their intelligent perusal will do more to clear away the mist of misunderstanding from the work of this literary group than can any form of argument. " What is

Popular Poetry ?'' asks Yeats, fresh from the study of those verse writers who had till then been considered representative: " I knew in my heart that most of them wrote badly, and yet such romance clung about them, such a desire for Irish poetry was in all our minds, that I kept on saying, not only to others but to myself, that most of them wrote well, or all but well . . . . I thought one day—I can remember the very day when I thought it—' If somebody could make a style, which would not be an English style, and yet would be musical and full of colour, many others would catch fire from him, and we would have a really great school of ballad poetry in Ireland. If those poets . . . . had a good tradition they would write beautifully, and move everybody as they move me . . . . If they had something else to write about besides political opinions, if more of them would write about the beliefs of the people, like Allingham, or about old legends like Ferguson, they would find it easier to get a style.' Then, with a deliberateness that still surprises me, for in my heart of hearts I have never been quite certain that one should be more than an artist, that even patriotism is more than an impure desire in an artist, I set to work to find a style . . . .''

Who can deny that Dr. Yeats's quest has been rewarded with success? But its slow and painful achievement illuminated certain points for him. " I had been busy a very little while before I knew that what we call popular poetry never came from the people at all. Longfellow, and Campbell, and Mrs. Hemans . . . . are the poets of the middle class . . . . the triviality of emotion, the poverty of ideas, the imperfect sense of beauty of a poetry whose most typical expression is Longfellow . . . . Go down into the street and read to your baker or your candlestick maker any poem which is not popular poetry . . . . or go down into the street with some thought whose bare meaning must be plain to everybody; take with you Ben Jonson's ' Beauty, like sorrow, dwelleth everywhere,' and find out how utterly its enchantment depends on an association of beauty with sorrow which written tradition has from the unwritten, which had it in its turn from ancient religion." This mistrust of any appreciative capacity upon the part of the baker and candlestick maker has in it, indeed, something of a prophetic strain, where Dr. Yeats and his colleagues were concerned; and his conclusion a little further on is significant, if a little unconvincing: "There is only one kind of good poetry, for the poetry of the coteries, which presupposes the written tradition, does not differ in kind from the true poetry of the people, which presupposes the unwritten tradition. Both are alike strange and obscure." I can indeed understand Dr. Yeats's solicitude to reconcile a democracy and aristocracy of verse: yet I fear facts may be held to have proved a little too much for him in this regard;

while I recognise a prose anticipation of that subsequent poetic satire at the expense of the middle class, yet another aspect of the poet's great disillusion :

> " *What need you, being come to sense,*
> *But fumble in a greasy till*
> *And add the half-pence to the pence*
> *And prayer to shivering prayer, until*
> *You have dried the marrow from the bone;*
> *For men were born to pray and save.*"

In his remarks upon *The Theatre* from which I have already quoted, this division of art as possessing two sources is again to be found : " The drama has need of cities that it may find men in sufficient numbers, and cities destroy the emotions to which it appeals, and therefore the days of the drama are brief, and come but seldom. It has one day when the emotions of cities still remember the emotions of sailors and husbandmen and shepherds and users of the spear and bow; . . . . and it has another day, now beginning, when thought and scholarship discover their desire. In the first day it is the Art of the people, and in the second day . . . . it is the preparation of a Priesthood." But the conclusion of this essay is not over-confident : " It will take . . . . perhaps generations to restore the Theatre of Art . . . . if one could call one's painters and one's actors from where one would, how easy it would be ! I know some painters who have never painted

82

scenery, who could paint the scenery I want, but they have their own work to do; and in Ireland I have heard a red-haired orator repeat some bad political verses with a voice that went through one like flame, and made them seem the most beautiful verses in the world; but he has no practical knowledge of the stage, and probably despises it."

That red-headed orator, unquestionably a member of the middle class, a baker or candlestick maker even, has surely much to answer for in recent and contemporary Irish history; but Dr. Yeats has enough perception to lead one to expect that he would have substituted the word *mistrusts* for *despises*.

It is, however, in *Ireland and the Arts*, from which I have already quoted freely, that one will find the fullest exposition of those ideals which Dr. Yeats had once hoped might become popular. Yet even this essay, so full of optimistic youth, opens ominously with the sentence: "The arts have failed; fewer people are interested in them every generation." But this is to be no deterrent.

"The Greeks, the only perfect artists of the world, looked within their own borders, and we, like them, have a history fuller than any modern history of imaginative events; and legends which surpass, as I think, all legends but theirs in wild beauty, and in our land, as in theirs, there is no river or mountain that is not associated in the memory with some event or legend . . . . I would

83

have our writers and craftsmen of many kinds master this history and these legends, and fix upon their memory the appearance of mountains and rivers, and make it all visible again in their arts . . . . In other words, I would have Ireland recreate the ancient arts, the arts as they were understood in Judea, in India, in Scandinavia, in Greece and Rome, in every ancient land; as they were understood when they moved a whole people, and not a few people who have grown up in a leisured class . . . . we all hope for arts like these."

Dr. Yeats has referred to the influence of William Morris in the composition of *The Secret Rose*, where personally I do not find it; but I perceive it very clearly in much of the foregoing. These aesthetic sentiments were surely unexceptionable even in Ireland, which possesses the touchiest public in the world; but the author presently proceeds to wear his rue with a difference: "I will not, however, have all my readers with me when I say that no writer, no artist, even though he choose Brian Boru or St. Patrick for his subject, should try to make his work popular. Once he has chosen a subject he must think of nothing but giving it such an expression as will please himself . . . . He must make his work a part of his own journey towards beauty and truth. He must picture saint, or hero, or hillside, as he sees them, not as he is expected to see them, and he must comfort himself, when others cry out against what he has seen, by remembering that no two men are alike, and that ' there is no excellent beauty without strangeness.' In this matter he must be without humility." Such an unrepentant individualism married to subjectivity could have but the one outcome with an Irish public : Was not the poet to later make the melancholy discovery that " all great art is essentially lonely " ? Yet how brave that far-off youthful impulse of thirty years ago ! Listen again, and judge the quality of Yeats's patriotism. " I cannot but believe that if our painters of Highland cattle and moss-covered barns were to care enough for their country to care for what makes it different from other countries they would discover, when struggling, it may be, to paint the exact grey of the bare Burren hills, and of a sudden it may be, a new style, their very selves . . . . I am yet jealous for Cuchulain, and for Baile, and for Aillinn, and for those grey mountains that still are lacking their celebration. I sometimes reproach myself because I cannot admire Mr. Hughes's beautiful, piteous *Orpheus and Eurydice* with an unquestioning mind. I say with my lips, ' The Spirit made it, for it is beautiful, and the Spirit bloweth where it listeth,' but I say in my heart, ' Aengus and Etain would have served his turn.' " If patriotism be not here, where may it be found? while for nobility and generosity what can surpass the closing period of the subsequent essay, entitled *The Galway Plains:* " To have even perfectly the thoughts that can be weighed, the knowledge that can be got from books, the precision that can be learned at school, to belong to any aristocracy, is to be a little pool that will soon dry up. A people alone are a great river . . . ." Much has been written concerning symbolism in connexion with Dr. Yeats: may there not be a symbolic element in that allusion to a circumscribed intellectual pool liable to evaporation? and has not that great river since swept by upon an unforeseen irresistible destructive course . . . .?

I have quoted at some length from those essays which have a more or less exclusively Irish content, but a large, if not the larger number deal significantly enough, perhaps, with matters of English literature and general aesthetics. *The Happiest of the Poets* treats of William Morris, whom the poet had known, and contains some penetrating criticism expressed in an individual style; as where he writes of the women characters of Morris: " They are not in love with love for its own sake, with a love that is apart from the world or at enmity with it, as Swinburne imagines Mary Stuart, and as all men have imagined Helen. They do not seek in love that ecstasy, which Shelley's nightingale called death, that extremity of life in which life seems to pass away like the phoenix in flame of its own lighting, but rather a gentle self-surrender that would lose more than half its sweetness if it lost the savour of coming

days." And again, how admirably he expresses
the faint cloying that comes upon the reader
under the influence of the monotony of Morris's
verse. "His poetry often wearies us as the un-
broken green of July wearies us, for there is
something in us, some bitterness because of the
Fall, it may be, that takes a little from the
sweetness of Eve's apple after the first mouthful;
but he who did all things gladly and easily,
who never knew the curse of labour, found it
always as sweet as it was in Eve's mouth." It
is in the final sentence of the essay that Dr. Yeats
entirely succeeds in compressing the artistic
temperament of a fellow-craftsman into a few
words, when he says of Morris: "He may not
have been, indeed he was not, among the very
greatest of the poets, but he was among the
greatest of those who prepare the last reconciliation when the Cross shall blossom with roses."
Passages such as these constitute an example of
criticism suffused with imaginative sympathy. It
is in *The Philosophy of Shelley's Poetry*, perhaps,
that Dr. Yeats has achieved the most elaborate,
the most rhapsodical effect with prose: certain
sentences occupy almost an entire page, containing
those parentheses within parentheses which render
the reading of such passages a little fatiguing;
I know of nothing comparable to this essay,
except certain writings of Walter Pater; and I
quote the conclusion as an example of a prose
style stretched almost to breaking point, like an

87

over-strung lute string, to emit ideas almost too tenuous for normal apprehension. " . . . . Shelley, who hated life, because he sought 'more in life than any understood,' would have wandered, lost in a ceaseless reverie, in some chapel of the star of infinite desire. I think, too, that as he knelt before an altar, where a thin flame burnt in a lamp made of green agate, a single vision would have come to him again and again, a vision of a boat drifting down a broad river between high hills where there were caves and towers, and following the light of one Star; and that voices would have told him how there is for every man some one scene, some one adventure, some one picture that is the image of his secret life, for wisdom first speaks in images, and that this one image, if he would but brood over it his life long, would lead his soul, disentangled from unmeaning circumstance and the ebb and flow of the world, into that far household, where the undying gods await all those whose souls have become simple as flame, whose bodies have become quiet as an agate lamp." All who are acquainted with Shelley's longer poems, such as *Alastor*, must admire this visionary synthesis of his life-long quest for Intellectual Beauty, his personal *itinerarium mentis ad Deum*, to whose prosecution, in spite of self-induced sorrow and suffering that ineffable spirit so obstinately clung. *The Symbolism of Poetry* is necessarily of particular interest in connexion with its author; but I propose to take from it only two brief extracts. Towards the conclusion Dr. Yeats expresses the opinion: "The form of sincere poetry . . . . unlike the form of the popular poetry . . . . must have the perfections that escape analysis, the subtleties that have a new meaning every day." This phrase, as a summation of that indefinable quality, that indissoluble blend of form, emotion and rhythm, exhibited by the best poetry, indeed by the best art of every kind, remains a perfect and ironic commentary upon all attempts to break a poetic butterfly upon the critical wheel. Earlier in this same essay he quotes from Goethe: "Goethe has said, a poet needs all philosophy, but he must keep it out of his work," adding "though that is not always necessary." I must confess that upon this particular point, at the risk of national disloyalty, I adhere to the Teuton rather than the Celt. For with the introduction of philosophy the death-knell of true lyric poetry sounded, I fear, for William Butler Yeats. Had he not exclaimed already in *Reconciliation* a love poem written during that tumult of his disillusion:

"*But dear, cling close to me: since you were gone,*
My barren thoughts have chilled me to the bone."

A cynical or malicious critic might claim the last line as a prophetic form of epitaph upon the poet's muse.

VI.

" Red Rose, sad Rose, proud Rose of all my days,
   Come near me " . . . .

sang the poet in his early phase; and in that rose, a type of the perfect abstract principle of Beauty, of which all beautiful forms and emotions are but partial manifestations, he gave to his readers a symbol not over-difficult to understand, while linking his philosophy, if indeed the term fittingly apply, to the inspiration of some of the greatest poets; to Shelley's *Hymn to Intellectual Beauty*, as to Keats's exposition, whose famous cadences conclude the *Ode on a Grecian Urn:*

" Beauty is Truth, Truth Beauty: that is all
   Ye know on Earth, and all ye need to know."

In later life, when settled in that tower which he had " decked and altered for a girl's love," he had provided, amongst its many amenities, as he tells us:

" An acre of stony ground,
   Where the symbolic Rose can break in flower."

I sometimes wonder if there is a self-conscious irony in that allusion to *stony ground;* too stony, alas, to permit of further blossoming upon the part of that transplanted rose. It has withered from his work, while Dr. Yeats has deliberately set himself to transgress Goethe's prescription that while a poet needs all philosophy he must carefully exclude it from his work.

" It seems that I must bid the Muse go pack,
Choose Plato and Plotinus for a friend
Until imagination, ear and eye,
Can be content with argument and deal
In abstract things."

Many of us find ourselves at a loss to understand this compulsion, more particularly when we find a little later, even Plato, Aristotle, and Pythagoras and their speculations epitomised as

" Old clothes upon old sticks to scare a bird."

Dr. Yeats, therefore, can hardly have undertaken his dreary excursion into the Arabian desert with his eyes otherwise than completely open as to the personal result.

I think it will be conceded that any philosophy to be tolerable must become to a greater or lesser extent humanised; thus Plato in his *Dialogues* controls, and will always control our consuming interest, because of the human personalities of Socrates and his companions, still speaking to us with living voices, which we can understand, across the centuries. St. Augustine, in his *Confessions*—the most perfect, the most complete exposition on record of the *itinerarium mentis ad Deum*, from which even Dr. Yeats finds himself compelled to quote, draws us on page after page of that spiritual masterpiece of masterpieces, from valley to ascent, and from ascent to peak of illumination by virtue of the warm human atmosphere suffusing his speculations. In a word, if philosophy be the pursuit of wisdom, and if wisdom be one of the attributes of deity, not without reason may the cynics exclaim that Man has made God in his own image and likeness. But The Mask, The Antithetical Self, with The Phases of the Moon, and the associated doctrine of rebirth impress me as inhuman, or dehumanised in their abstruseness, while in regard to their application to character of the lunar cycle, which Dr. Yeats expounds so laboriously, and at such length, I think it inevitably reflects its chilly source in that planet which astronomers assure us is dead and frozen. One practical application I find in this preoccupation with The Phases of the Moon: it turns upon a supposed correspondence between the lunar period and the temperament of the individual born under that period; commensurate with the phase is the relative proportion of subjectivity and objectivity in that person's mentality. Hence my thesis, that Dr. Yeats's life-long work contains evidence of a struggle for adjustment between these two elements in his own nature, finds support from the scheme of speculation which involves him so much to the detriment, if not absorption, of his poetic faculty. Mr. Schulyer Jackson in his admirable essay upon Yeats, published many years ago in *The London*

Mercury, alludes to the conflict in the poet between " his sense of living, and his sense of life "— which I take to be a more academic and elaborate phrasing for subjective and objective.

I have had already the temerity to suggest that Dr. Yeats's sense of humour is not developed in equal proportion with his other high mental faculties: even if true, this need not, and indeed will not, distress Dr. Yeats, for the same deficiency has been counted against Milton and Shelley. I am persuaded that this practical lack is responsible for *The Celtic Twilight:* it emerges again in certain places, even in *Ideas of Good and Evil*, noticeably in the essay entitled *Magic*, with its uncomfortable suggestion which causes Dr. Yeats's pursuit of the supernatural to resemble vaguely the trustful awe of a child at an old-fashioned children's party, presided over by a conjuror, hired for those juvenile guests' entertainment, as he draws the rabbit from his breeches pocket, and causes the egg to miraculously disappear. Nothing else can credibly account for Dr. Yeats's foregathering with Madame Blavatsky, that acknowledged charlatan, and exposed impostress, than an incapacity to laugh at himself or at others: and its final liability, let us hope, consists in The Phases of the Moon. I have had, may I say, the privilege of seeing performances of three out of the *Four Plays for Dancers*—namely, *At the Hawk's Well, The Only Jealousy of Emer*, and *The Dreaming of the*

Bones: as an entirely new art form I consider these productions incomparable, in their complete conveyance of an indefinable emotion: and I like best the last mentioned, which contains least of esotericism, and consider it, in effect, Dr. Yeats's unquestioned masterpiece. But in the notes to this unique book are contained a mixture of obscurity and preciosity unworthy of so great an artist as the author. Kusta Ben Luki, with his companions among the Judwalis of Arabia Deserta remind me in a most uncomfortable way of those modifications of the Genii contained in the *Arabian Nights Entertainments*, whose emergence at the supreme moment from a trap-door in the stage, furnishes an infantile thrill at a performance, say, of the pantomime of Aladdin. In the notes on *Calvary*, however, a certain elderly Arab is described who is surely the apotheosis of a misdirected solemnity. This individual, as one would expect, is characterised as " the votary of a small contentious sect," and upon his death-bed proceeds to an exposition of his general outlook upon human life and its vicissitudes, concluding with the statement: " Because it is very difficult, and because I have put my understanding into three songs, I am famous among my people." One would hardly expect so entirely intolerable an intellectual snob with his trinity of lyrics to inhabit the Arabian desert; one would rather presume to find him in some little self-sufficient clique of half-educated ultra-modern

94

persons : some circumscribed intellectual pool liable to early if not immediate evaporation; and some at all events, will be disappointed at the serious consideration given him by one who could prefix to his own work the lyric cry of St. Augustine, with its universality and sanity of aspiration: *Sero te amavi, Pulchritudo tam antiqua et tam nova! Sero te amavi!*

Not content with these notes, Dr. Yeats has written an entire erudite volume upon the subject : and in the verse epilogue which concludes it, has woven, perhaps unwittingly, a winding-sheet for the precious and obscure :

*" I have mummy truths to tell
Whereat the living mock . . . .
Such thought, that in it bound
I need no other thing
Wound in mind's wandering,
As mummies in the mummy-cloth are wound."*

May not the truly living, after all, possess a justification for mockery? Is it again an imperfect sense of humour, or a tragic pose, which has induced Dr. Yeats to employ that unfortunate image of a mummy? A mummy, which, no matter how it may have preserved the form of what once was living, is, in spite of that resemblance and associated superstition, quintessentially dead. Inanimate and cold, for all its jewelled, perfumed wrappings as are the frozen mountains of the moon, no matter what her transitory phase.

In that poem from *The Tower* entitled *Meditations in Time of Civil War*, from which I have quoted that passage so expressive of Dr. Yeats's sense of intellectual isolation, the poet turning from the doorway concludes with an attempt at personal consolation:

> " *The abstract joy,*
> *The half-read wisdom of daemonic images,*
> *Suffice the ageing man as once the growing boy.*"

I personally detect a faint resemblance between the state of mind depicted here, and that of the child who passes through the churchyard at midnight, and who whistles to assure himself that he is not afraid; while, if Dr. Yeats desires to justify himself, I regard the adjective " half-read " as possibly unfortunate. I am more than ever persuaded that Dr. Yeats is at heart dissatisfied with his mental conclusions: is there not a somewhat plaintive note in the concluding paragraph from that disappointing and inconclusive metaphysical volume, *Per Amica Silentia Lunae?*

> " As I go up and down my stair and pass the gilded Moorish wedding-chest where I keep my ' barbarous words,' I wonder will I take to them once more . . . . or, now that I shall in a little be growing old, to some kind of simple piety like that of an old woman."

The poet might possibly do worse, for

such a simplicity would not be inconsistent after
all with intellectual dignity; indeed, if dignity
alone be in question, who would not prefer for
Dr. Yeats the stark negation of Sophocles which
he renders with such exquisite perfection in his
adaptation of *Oedipus at Colonus:*

> "*In the long echoing street the laughing dancers
> throng,
> The bride is carried to the bridegroom's chamber
> through torchlight and tumultuous song;
> I celebrate the silent kiss that ends short life or
> long.*
>
> *Never to have lived is best, ancient writers say;
> Never to have drawn the breath of life, never
> to have looked into the eye of day;
> The second best's a gay good-night and quickly
> turn away.*"

As I read many of the later poems, weighted
with a confused burden of Oriental and Christian
mysticism, I am reminded of what Walter Pater
has written concerning Pico Della Mirandola, his
"ambitious array of every sort of learning, a
profuse imagery borrowed from the astrologers,
the Cabala, and Homer, and Sophocles, and
Dionysius the Areopagite"; and where in the
notes to *Four Plays for Dancers*, repeated allusion
is made to those mysterious, and, it may be,
mythical Robartes papers which the poet declares
have provided him with all the philosophy he
needs, I am again reminded of a further
observation from that admirable essay in *The*

Renaissance : " It is said," writes Pater, " that Pico, in his eagerness for mysterious learning, once paid a great sum for a collection of cabalistic manuscripts, which turned out to be forgeries; and the story might well stand as a parable of all he ever seemed to gain in the way of actual knowledge." A melancholy comparison thus far, though in many eyes a flattering one; nevertheless I take comfort from that remark of Yeats already quoted concerning his possible return to an old woman's piety, a return which incidentally would complete his intellectual resemblance to Pico Della Mirandola, who, as Pater also tells us, died " amid the prayers and sacraments of Savonarola . . . ." " an instance," he elsewhere contends, " of those who, after following the vain hope of an impossible reconciliation from system to system, have at last fallen back unsatisfied on the simplicity of their childhood's belief."

VII.

EGOISM is usually distasteful in the adult; while egoism in the child is natural and permissible; for which reason few, if any, will carp at *Reveries over Childhood and Youth*. Moreover, Dr. Yeats's self-absorption at that early age was of a type generally familiar from our knowledge of other over-sensitive children, who, however abnormal we may consider them individually, nevertheless exhibit practically uniform symptoms. Thus Dr.

Yeats writes that he was unhappy as a child, and without reason; and further that he confused his grandfather with God; thereby manifesting that anthropomorphic instinct recognisable in other children of genius; notably in William Blake, who, at a similar early age, believed that he saw God put his forehead to the window. " I remember little of childhood," declares Dr. Yeats, " but its pain . . . . certainly my miseries were not made by others, but *were a part of my own mind.*" From which remark one may reasonably infer that the child in this particular instance, was father to the man, in Wordsworth's hackneyed phrase. So many traits and characteristics were apparently present in the germ, that one regrets that this volume, with its individual flavour, and peculiar capacity to arouse interest over trifles, must of necessity have been written in maturity, lest possibly the author should unconsciously refer to the past origins and foundation for the present which had no positive existence at the time. One feels, at moments, that the only veracious auto-biography of a child should be written, if such a procedure were possible, during the period of childhood itself. Thus we learn that while at school in Hammersmith, whither his family had removed from Sligo, Dr. Yeats " followed the career of a certain professional runner for months . . . . I had seen him described as the *bright particular star of American athletics*, and the wonderful phrase had thrown enchantment over him. Had he been called the *particular bright star*, I should have cared nothing for him. I did not understand the symptom for years after." An instinct for verbal arrangement was subsequently to develop into a sense of style. Again, we learn upon one occasion, "I have climbed to the top of a tree by the edge of the playing field, and am looking at my schoolfellows, and am as proud of myself as a March cock when it crows to its first sunrise. I am saying to myself: 'If, when I grow up I am as clever among grown up men as I am among these boys, I shall be a famous man.' I remind myself how they think all the same things and cover the school walls at election times with the opinions their fathers find in the newspapers. I remind myself that I am an artist's son, and must take some work as the whole end of life, and not think as the others do of becoming well-off and living pleasantly." All of which, while to-day partaking of the nature of prophecy happily fulfilled, goes to show that even at a tender age, Dr. Yeats was not entirely devoid of self-consciousness and self-confidence, not to hint at a suspicion of priggishness.

His loyalty to his connexion, and to his father in particular, may not be questioned, and is admirable: for he is content to quote his father against himself, perhaps unconsciously. "Ideals," remarked John Butler Yeats upon one occasion, "make the blood thin, and take the human nature out of people," and upon another occasion he observed that " all contemplative men were in a conspiracy to overrate their state of life, and all writers are of them, excepting the *great poets*." A not unreasonable inference from these comments might be that ideals, and contemplation, equivalent terms for subjectivity, may result in an impaired sense of humour and proportion. Nevertheless the son in this particular instance, did not permit an affectionate admiration to modify his own individual point of view. " Personal utterance," he had come to the conclusion, " which had almost ceased in English literature, could be as fine an escape from rhetoric and abstraction as drama itself. My father was indignant, almost violent, and would hear of nothing but drama. 'Personal utterance,' he declared, 'was only egotism.'" In view of those poems of Dr. Yeats's middle period from which I have so freely quoted, I for one rejoice that father and son failed to see eye to eye in this matter; nevertheless, I regret that, while personal utterance has exonerated the poet from rhetoric, it does not appear to have completely eliminated a tendency to abstraction; a fact which is rendered the more remarkable by his apparent knowledge of the danger, and anxiety to avoid it. The actual biographical details in *Reveries* are relatively unimportant; but at the conclusion, Dr. Yeats succeeds to a universality of expression sufficiently rare in his case to justify transcription: " When

I think of all the books I have read, and of the
wise words I have heard spoken, and of the
anxiety I have given to parents and grandparents,
and of the hopes that I have had, all life, weighed
in the scales of my own life, seems to me a
preparation for something that never happens."
That, as Matthew Arnold would express it, is
admirably said: a preparation for something that
never happens, but whose vague expectation, one
might add, provides us with a justification for
continued existence.

The Trembling of the Veil constitutes the direct
sequel to *Reveries*: it is of immeasurably superior
interest, owing to the appearance in its pages
of people whose position in art and letters has
since become established; but I consider the book
as definitely deficient in good taste, and in the
original edition, at all events, slightly slovenly
in style. The author must have foreseen the
possibility of some such criticism, since in the
foreword he states: " I have not felt my freedom
abated, for most of the friends of my youth are
dead, and over the dead I have an historian's
right . . . .I have said all the good I know, and
all the evil: I have kept nothing back necessary
to understanding." There is a popular phrase
that it is never what one says that matters, but
the way one says it; which expresses perfectly the
grounds of my dissatisfaction with Dr. Yeats's
disclosures: they convey to me a disagreeable
impression that his relations with those brilliant

and frequently unhappy men, members of *The Rhymers' Club* for the most part, whom he categorises as *The Tragic Generation*, were unsympathetic and detached: that he watched their disastrous progress with a keen eye for future potential " copy," his attitude savouring more of the scientific than the humanistic: above all, in the name of common decency, one is surely justified in entering a protest against a certain infamous episode recounted concerning Oscar Wilde. There is a considerable amount of wit scattered throughout these pages: as where Stepniak, the Nihilist, complained of Henley's Sunday evening symposia: " I cannot go there more than once a year—it is too exhausting," an opinion that the average man would be likely to endorse: and where Wilde is reported as remarking that " Mr. George Bernard Shaw has no enemies, but is intensely disliked by all his friends," a statement which is probably strictly accurate: or where O'Leary is quoted as saying: " no gentleman can be a socialist—but he might be an anarchist." The wit does not consist solely of quotations, and the *jeux d'esprit* of others, much of it is Dr. Yeats's own, but in nearly every instance it is a little unkind, dare one say a little feline, when exhibited towards his fellows. He does not, however, always spare himself, as when in connexion with certain literary organisations he states that he " began to feel that he needed a hostess more than a society, but that he was not to find for years to come." Possibly the most obvious of his thrusts at others is when, having witnessed *Arms and the Man* (which he disliked) for the first time, he had a nightmare that he was "haunted by a sewing machine, that clicked and shone, but the incredible thing was that the machine smiled, smiled perpetually." Few dare deny that Mr. George Bernard Shaw clicks, shines, and continually smiles, a literary combination which an undazzled yet enlightened posterity may decide does not, after all, constitute the highest form of dramatic art. Furthermore, from prolonged meditation upon affairs, Dr. Yeats attains at moments to something of a prophetic strain, as when he asked one night at the Hotel Corneille: "After Mallarmé, after Paul Verlaine, after Gustave Moreau, after Puvis de Chavannes, after our own verse, after all our subtle colour and nervous rhythm, after the faint mixed tints of Conder, what more is possible?" concluding with the terrible answer, which all Western Europe dreads, in other spheres than Art: "After us, the Savage God." Again, some of us cannot but admire and in disheartened moments temporarily subscribe to his summation of the Irish National Movement from the foundation of the Land League to the present day: "A movement, first of poetry, then of sentimentality and land hunger, had struggled with, and, as the nation passed into the second period of all revolutions, had given way before a movement

of abstraction and hatred : and after some twenty
years of the second period though abstraction and
hatred have won their victory, there is no clear
sign of a third, a *tertium quid* and a reasonable
frame of mind."

The Trembling of the Veil, together with
Reveries over Childhood and Youth constitute
explicit autobiography : there remain those
vestiges of implicit autobiography, those inevitable projections into literary form of the inner or
subjective life. Dr. Yeats in these pages characterises subjective men as " those who must spin
a web out of their own bowels " ; in *Wheels and
Butterflies* he completes, perhaps unconsciously,
his own portrait, when he writes of the " mind of
a man . . . . intellectualising, systematising, until
at last it lies dead, a spider smothered in its own
web." The poet's early preoccupation with
Parnell, that stern tragic solitary figure, was
significant enough ; his later interest in Swift I
consider more significant still, as evidenced in
particular in *The Words upon the Window Pane*,
that late blossoming of his art, which once more
gave the lie to those who eagerly emphasised
that for William Butler Yeats : " The rest is
silence." I suggest that his intellectual progress
from a belief in a democratic culture to what one
might term an aesthetic autocracy affords a
curious and interesting parallel with the political
trend in contemporary Europe ; and that his
career provides an endorsement, perhaps uncon-

scious, of Dr. Stockman's melancholy discovery
that, " The strongest man in the world is the
man who stands most alone." The image of Dr.
Yeats which remains indelibly imprinted upon my
own imagination is not the youthful figure, with
the extravagant neckwear and coiffure of Sargent's
almost perfect if idealised charcoal sketch, the
unsophisticated bird-like triller of *The Lake Isle
of Innisfree*: it is rather the stern, partly con-
ventionalised personality which looks out from
the later photographic portraits, with sombre eyes,
and close-set lips, from which, for all that they
are close-set, I can hear issuing the oppressive
mordant phrases from *Remorse for Intemperate
Speech*:

> " *I ranted to the knave and fool,*
> *But outgrew that school,*
> *Would transform the part,*
> *Fit audience found, but cannot rule*
> *My fanatic heart . . . .*
>
> *Out of Ireland have we come.*
> *Great hatred, little room,*
> *Maimed us at the start.*
> *I carry from my mother's womb*
> *A fanatic heart.*"

Subjectivity has had its triumph : what is there
here but the inevitable outcome for an introvert
flung into a whirlpool of extroversion, of that far-
off piteous cry of Aleel in *The Countess Cathleen?*

> " *Impetuous heart, be still, be still :*
> *Your sorrowful love may never be told ;*
> *Cover it up with a lonely tune.*"

106

CONCLUSION.

Unity of Being is a phrase much in Dr. Yeats's mouth, as likewise upon the lips of many of his more learned critics, who deplore that he has failed to attain the spiritual or psychological condition embodied in the phrase. I should prefer, for reasons of simplicity, to consider the poet as being the subject of incomplete self-realisation, which, as an inevitable result, renders him lacking in universality. The cause of this imperfect self-expression is a matter for legitimate speculation: I have my own suspicions as to its nature which I have presumed to hint at. A consideration of Dr. Yeats's most vital, most personal work, would lead me, at all events, if I might coin a phrase, to describe him as " the poet of frustration and isolation." I never read certain poems of his without vividly recalling those ludicrously dissimilar verses of Robert Browning's entitled *Youth and Art:*

" *It once might have been, once only:*
We lodged in a street together,
You, a sparrow on the housetop lonely,
I, a lone she-bird of his feather . . . .

We studied hard in our styles,
Chipped each at a crust like Hindoos,
For air looked out on the tiles,
For fun watched each other's windows . . . .

107

Could you say so, and never say,
'Suppose we join hands and fortunes
And I fetch her from over the way?' . . . .

No, no; you would not be rash,
Nor I rasher, and something over . . . .

Each life unfulfilled, you see;
It hangs still, patchy and scrappy;
We have not sighed deep, laughed free,
Starved, feasted, despaired—been happy.

And nobody calls you a dunce,
And people suppose me clever:
This could but have happened once,
And we missed it, lost it for ever."

Now, in those contrasting and contradictory
words, " starved, feasted, despaired—been
happy," lies the secret, the key to the mystery
of great and universal poetry. Shakespeare,
holding horses outside the London inns; Dante,
forever exiled from the mistress of his soul,
Beatrice, as from the mistress of his mind,
Florence : Keats struggling in the meshes of
passion and consumption : Francis Thompson
derelict in the streets, with opium for consolation :
all these saw through their experience into the
heart of things, to find therein the nobility, the
strength, the universality of great poetry. They
cast all their bread upon the bitter waters of
affliction, withholding no niggardly crumb for
reasons of circumspection, human respect or
prudence : and the Muses accepted their sacrifice,

and Apollo crowned them with the unfading laurel. Even Wordsworth, whom Dr. Yeats describes as "after a brief blossoming, sawn into obviously utilitarian planks," to some extent took his life in his hands in revolutionary Paris, where he was, moreover, guilty of an indiscretion not usually associated with meanness of disposition, timidity of spirit, or mere expediency. None of these men during their lifetime, foregathered within the narrow limits of expository societies: least of all can any of them be conceived as desiring a hostess. Even Browning himself, successful wealthy citizen of the world, and unwilling victim of an explanatory coterie though he became, rose to the one supreme occasion of his life like a man: when he bore away the pining valetudinarian prisoner from her narrow Victorian horsehair sofa with that exclamation of such characteristic virile simplicity: "If my heart's wish avail, you shall laugh yet at east winds as I do."

I make so bold, then, as to conclude that Dr. Yeats is lacking in depth of human experience; his conflict being largely, if not invariably, intellectual and limited: I think that he has possibly written a little too much: I presume to suggest that success came to him a little too readily; I consider that he either misunderstood or underestimated certain contemporary movements in Ireland, and that, as a result of all these factors

109

his own mental position is in something of the nature of an intellectual *cul-de-sac*. I have a private, personal, very probably quite inaccurate suspicion that he went around the corner upon more than one occasion to avoid his angel, which is the exact reverse of Mr. Schulyer Jackson's claim that no one has more consistently wrestled with that spiritual functionary: but then our individual interpretations of the phrase may be slightly at variance: and the sum total of these facts, as I believe, pulls his art down from the higher level to which it might otherwise have attained. The most universal, if not the only universal line of Dr. Yeats which I can recall is that from *Ephemera:*

" *Our souls are love, and a continual farewell.*"

In the hands of a universal poet such as Dante, or even the less universal Shelley, that line would become endowed with a vast comprehensive significance: but I remember that Dr. Yeats has only employed it in relation to the evanescence of mere physical passion. Although Dr. Yeats has quoted St. Augustine, and dabbles in mystical theology, I never find in his writing a final definitive axiomatic line such as that of Dante concerning Deity:

" *In His will is our peace.*"

While the title of mystic is claimed for him, I never find anything comparable to the titanic phrase of that otherwise very minor poet Vaughan:

> " *There is in God, some say,*
> *A deep but dazzling darkness.*"

And above all I miss in him completely that sense of sympathy with suffering human flesh and blood which inspires his erstwhile contemporary Francis Thompson to exclaim that:

> " *We are born in other's pain*
> *And perish in our own.*"

Mr. Forrest Reid, in a long, careful, and discriminating study of Dr. Yeats, concludes by comparing him to Milton; a comparison quite beyond my imperfect comprehension. In his early lyric work, in such poems as *The Two Trees*, I would pay Dr. Yeats the supreme compliment of finding no comparison with any other English poet possible: while in that group of poems dedicated to " intellectual love," I hasten to pay him the equivalent compliment of a comparison with Donne: Donne of *The Anniversary*, or *The Triple Fool*,—or *The Relic;* and if the comparison carries with it a suggestion of limitation, a lack of universality, most of us would be willing to be limited if Donne were chairman of that limited company: moreover, has not Dr. Yeats himself expressed the pious and possibly penetrating hope that:

> " *I may dine at journey's end*
> *With Landor and with Donne* "?

If the hereafter is to consist of a glorification of such old-fashioned social usage as the dinner party, and if I were privileged to act in the capacity of celestial waiter, I certainly would set entirely apart a table for three: where I would lay a cover for Donne, Landor and Yeats, confident that I had seated together three unique artists of exquisite technique, but limited appeal.

There is a phrase, a melancholy phrase, I think, of French origin: that to travel is better than to arrive. I shall lay aside my pen sadly conscious of the force of these words. To Dr. William Butler Yeats I owe a debt, a double, it may well be an irredeemable debt: one half he has assuredly forgotten: of the other half he must necessarily be ignorant: in undertaking this essay, I was animated by the hope that I might partially, at least, discharge that heavy obligation: but it is so weighty that I fear I may have failed. Yet should the illustrious subject of these pages ever come across them, which is unlikely, or desire to read them, which is possibly less likely still, I would recommend them to his courtesy and forbearance with the compassionate words of the Angel in *The Countess Cathleen*, words not only filled with human pity, but replete, for all that I have argued to the contrary, with universality of appeal:

> . . . . *The Light of Lights*
> *Looks always on the motive, not the deed;*
> *The Shadow of Shadows, on the deed alone.*"